IN SICILY

NORMAN LEWIS

IN SICILY

THOMAS DUNNE BOOKS
St. Martin's Press ⚏ New York

THOMAS DUNNE BOOKS.
An imprint of St. Martin's Press.

IN SICILY. Copyright © 2000 by Norman Lewis. All rights reserved.
Printed in the United States of America. No part of this book may be used
or reproduced in any manner whatsoever without written permission except
in the case of brief quotations embodied in critical articles or reviews. For
information, address St. Martin's Press, 175 Fifth Avenue,
New York, N.Y. 10010.

www.stmartins.com

ISBN 0-312-29048-9

First published in Great Britain by Jonathan Cape
Random House Group Limited

First U.S. Edition: June 2002

10 9 8 7 6 5 4 3 2 1

This book is dedicated to the memory of my dear friend Marcello Cimino, who, at the head of the drive by Sicilian journalists against the power of the Mafia, was to suffer a counter-attack in which his office was partially demolished by a bomb.

It also offers tribute to the work of Marcello's wife, Giuliana Saladino, author of *Terra Sangrienta*, possibly the most important study of the Mafia and the most moving account of its victims to date.

I

MY EARLY FASCINATION with things Sicilian grew
from a close acquaintance with Ernesto Corvaja, in
whose London house I lived for several years and whose
daughter Ernestina I had married. He was a man of the
south in exile, with watchful eyes beneath heavy lids
and whose skin, wherever exposed, had turned grey
through deprivation of the sun. This, he told me, had
happened quite suddenly within weeks of arriving in
Britain and an attempt to remedy the situation by the
use of a sun-lamp had been a failure. He spoke English
fluently, except for some difficulty in pronouncing the
letter h – thus the word 'hook', as he spoke it, became
'wook'. On arriving in London he had been to a tailor
in Conduit Street for advice as to how he should dress
to pass as an Englishman, and from that time on he
wore a dark blue pin-stripe suit every day. We got on
extremely well, although I resisted his efforts to make
me wear pin-stripe suits as well.

I met Ernesto shortly before the outbreak of the war,
which was declared while Ernestina and I were on holiday

visiting friends in the Americas. All British nationals were recommended by our embassy in Washington not to return by sea because of the possibility of an immediate U-boat attack on shipping, so Ernestina began what proved to be a long stay in the New World, while I returned to England, and continued to live with the Corvajas.

Ernesto spoke little of his origins. An ancestor, Prince Corvaja, had bought his princedom (one of 147) in Sicily from the Spanish Crown for 2,000 scudi in the eighteenth century. The Corvajas had in addition owned one of the island's fearful sulphur mines, in which children as young as five were driven under the whip to scrape up the sulphur through passages too narrow to admit an adult.

Of the twenty years Ernesto had spent in the United States little was revealed, although when I brought the subject up he agreed he had been a member of the Unione Siciliana, an organization he explained as engaged in charitable work in connection with the many virtually penniless immigrants arriving in America from his home country. A rumour that he had eventually been deported from the States was never confirmed. By the time I knew him he had become a professional gambler, playing cards each year for three months in the casino at Ostend, where he was generally referred to among the players as the 'Monsieur Anglais'. It was a profession that bored him, and tied to it for three months at a time he was increasingly repelled by the shallowness and crudity of the environment.

As a boy Ernesto had been taken by an uncle with antiquarian interests on a visit to a number of Sicily's historic sites where excavations among Roman, Greek and even earlier settlements had revealed evidence of a magnificent past. It was only when the strong black wine imported by the cask from his old country loosened his tongue that the memories of these experiences exerted themselves. He had watched spellbound while specialist grave-robbers cleaned figurines from Morgantina – famous for moving their eyes – and had marvelled at a jewelled bull from Mesopotamia and a necklace that had adorned the throat of a courtesan or princess of the time of Philip of Macedon. Ernesto had approached his father to ask if he could train as a museum curator at Palermo or Rome, but he was sent off to Berne to take a degree in law, and in the end lived by shuffling and dealing out cards and thus lost sight of the brilliance of the past.

In the several years in which I lived in Ernesto's London house I can remember only a single reference made to his active life as a young man in Sicily. This concerned an occasion when he had agreed to become the second of a friend who had been challenged to a duel by one of the celebrated swordsmen of his day. Both were rich young men with too much time on their hands and given to brutal sports and the practice of unpleasant jokes. Starving cats were captured in the streets of Palermo and taken to the Parco della Favorita to be hunted down and eventually killed by young horsemen using steel-tipped whips. Another sport was to capture and strip black African immigrants, take them to the park and douse them in tubs of whitewash kept in readiness there.

It was in this romantically wild and still beautiful place that Palermo's duels were fought, and here Ernesto drove in his carriage accompanying his young friend Armando Mostella. Mostella's challenger, Angelo D'Alema, had killed nine opponents in a single year. The drawback with Palermo, Ernesto admitted, was that there were far too many rich young men with little else to do with their lives than defend their supposed honour, and the statistics of violent death responded to a fatal over-sensitivity in alliance with pride.

Armando's refusal to apologize for 'incivility' – he had pushed past D'Alema in the struggle to enter Palermo's cathedral when the doors were flung open on Easter Day – had led to the quarrel. By local standards it was his right to call on Ernesto's support in this crisis, since both men had been baptized in the font of the Duomo of Catania on the same day, and thus linked by an indestructible bond.

Ernesto recalled his doubts as to the likely outcome of the encounter. His friend would be fighting a duel for the first time, and his physical fitness was in decline due to a self-indulgent life. He had little to defend himself with but his courage. Ernesto had made a secret approach to the *maresciallo* (sergeant-major) of the police of the area, calling upon him to arrest the combatants on a charge of unlawful activity, but the man had refused, saying, 'The more they kill each other the better it is for us.'

Ernesto's heart sank as D'Alema's carriage rolled into sight through the trees. D'Alema was smiling. He remained seated when the carriage stopped. His second stepped down and Ernesto went to join him. D'Alema's man read out the formal complaint to which Ernesto replied with the usual sentence of five words. The weapons to be used, which were daggers of identical design and about eight inches in length, were then exhibited. The duellists spent a minute or two making small adjustments to the species of uniform they wore which provided some small protection in the shape of leather pads over the heart, the testicles and throat. They then saluted their seconds, and Armando, rooted to the spot, stood staring down at his knife as though it were some dreadful gift that had been forced upon him. D'Alema, his smile spreading, advanced to the attack.

Ernesto said that the speed of the final operation took him by surprise. D'Alema moved in quite close to Armando as if to initiate an intimate conversation, then struck a sudden blow low down in the body that curved round the perimeter of Armando's stomach, and his white shirt opened in a circular flap to lay bare a pink complex of intestines.

With this Ernesto went into action. He was wearing for the occasion one of the new bowler hats imported from England, and removing this he rushed to clamp it over Armando's stomach, and with an inch or two of entrail still showing under the brim, he manhandled his friend back into the carriage. A priest, previously warned of what was about to happen, came peddling up on his bicycle from a nearby hamlet, but was assured by Ernesto – a connoisseur by then of acts of violence – that it was not an occasion for the last rites.

And this was the case. It was possible, Ernesto believed, that even D'Alema could not bring himself to sacrifice this wholly defenceless victim in an action that would have added nothing to his lustre. D'Alema, said Ernesto, was shortly to be removed from the scene by sudden death. A car he had been driving in one of the early races round the winding Sicilian roads crashed on a sharp bend then fell into the sea, the general opinion being that someone had tampered with the brakes.

2

IT TURNED OUT, as the war got under way, that I was the possessor of a linguistic qualification at that time in some small demand. While on a journey in Southern Arabia I had picked up a smattering of Arabic which I hoped to improve by taking a course at the School of Oriental and African Studies in London. Before this could be completed I was asked to call at an address somewhere in the West End where it was suggested that I might be able to put my few words of Arabic to good use by joining the Intelligence Corps. The plan was that I should be set ashore from a submarine somewhere on the North African coast, and transmit intelligence back to London.

To prepare for this adventure I was packed off to the Intelligence Corps depot at Winchester, where after many days of ceremonial marching, three weeks were deemed necessary to convert applicants for all kinds of intelligence duties into expert motorcyclists. Squad after squad of trainees, mounted on ancient and often defective machines, were taken to the top of a steep grassy hill on the city's outskirts down which they hurtled, brakes disconnected, into a field at the bottom where the ambulance awaited.

In this I was carried off to Winchester Hospital with a caved-in chest where a handlebar had almost pushed its way through. It turned out that Ernesto was officially my next of kin, and I awoke next day to find him by my bed. The London traffic was in disarray through heavy bombing, but, notified of what had happened, he had rushed out of the house, found a taxi that could be bribed to take him to Winchester, and despite closed roads and detours to avoid craters and collapsed buildings, he was there in three hours. Seeing him sitting by my bed, I remembered the moment when his daughter, with myself in tow, had marched into his house to announce that we were married. The opaque eyes were fixed on me. Not a muscle moved in that imperturbable face in indication of what was going on in his head. 'Give me the paper,' he said in an even voice. He read it and I noticed a slight convulsion in the throat. This was known to Sicilians as 'swallowing the claws of the toad'. He then said, 'I'll give you my blood.' At the time I took this as no more than a conventional and meaningless Mediterranean formality, but now, in Winchester Hospital, I knew that it was not.

When the shattered bones had knitted up, I rejoined such of my comrades-in-arms as the motorcycles had spared to be despatched overseas. There we would confront military adventures for which we were imperfectly prepared. I went briefly to the Middle East, then to the Gulf, escorted three thousand Russians captured in German uniform back to their home country and spent a total of eighteen months in southern Italy. There we were in close contact with the Corps' Sicilian section in Palermo and swapped visits with them whenever we could. This enabled me to send Ernesto news of his own country and I learned from him that he had decided to return home as soon as he could. His house in London had been heavily damaged in an air raid, which had turned all the buildings on the opposite side of the road to rubble. He was hoping, he wrote, as soon as the war came to an end to return to the scenes of his youth in Taormina and Catania. In the meanwhile he was sounding out the possibility of buying a house in Aci Trezza, a beauty spot on the coast some five miles from Catania itself. Of this he would be interested to have news, he said, and I made an excuse to visit the place, suspecting at first sight that nothing much would have changed since he was last there.

Aci Trezza was a beautiful place but a little unearthly as it lay in the shadow of Mount Etna, with vast lava fields sloping towards it. Etna was said to influence both the appearance and personality of the people of such villages. The menfolk were taller and more handsome than their neighbours, and had the reputation of being more forthright in their dealings, and the women were famous for dowries that were richer than elsewhere. The pale shadows cast from the great peak brought out unexpected colours in the landscape. It was raining on the day I arrived and the water was jostling everywhere in the village. Green bubbles floated like uncut emeralds down every ditch. The sweep of the wind had left broom marks in the fresh snow and all the men in the streets had mourning shadows under their eyes.

I wrote back to London: 'You ask about the famous boats, and they're there as ever, with angels and flowers painted all over them. The big eruption hasn't changed anything except they have built churches these days with black and white lava. A village just down the coast was wiped out. The fishermen live in little round houses now, just like Africans. Nobody was killed and they've painted pictures of their saint on the rocks with arrows pointing away from the village to show which way the lava has to flow next time there's an eruption. Would you like to live here again? The answer is you're older now and that has to be taken into consideration. Probably yes – and so would I. Another thing is Catania has kept up with the times. They've actually opened a gambling saloon. You'd be in your element.'

I became so enchanted by the charm and the colour of the place that I borrowed a motorbike and decided to add a few days to my leave by exploring more of the area.

Everyone living under a volcano is affected by it whether they know it or not. Land is cheap and the work hard. They farm the fertile ground lying at the bottom of crevices and ravines, where, over three centuries, the lava has turned into good soil. Those who work this land look like Andean peones, with short legs, wide shoulders, high cheekbones, sleek black hair, and hands twice the normal size.

A cluster of roads led north from Catania and for the first few miles, until the lava came into sight, the going was easy. The lava fields, spreading over thirty-five miles, took my breath away. Many of those who had settled within fifteen miles of the city had bought land on the cheap, turning themselves into respected landowners. They had the famous Catanian sense of humour and they all laughed at nothing most of the time. 'If you're rich' – at least so they said – 'you have to plant palms around your house' – this being the local status symbol. They liked to point out that they were unlikely to live long enough to enjoy the fruit.

A few miles further north, with the volcano now in permanent view, the going became less easy, with narrower roads and sometimes diversions to avoid a recent lava flow. A cloud resembling in shape a Tudor flat hat hung above the cone of Etna and you could pick out fresh lava trails by the smoking vegetation. It was a landscape that demolished assumptions. You expected a white wilderness, whereas what you saw were narrow ravines crowded with wildflowers of every conceivable colour, which scented the surroundings with a perfume penetrating even the sulphurous fumes of the lava.

At Zafferana, quite near the crater, the local doctor specialized in nervous disorders. He told me he treated his patients by making them wear nothing but red clothing. If a house was wiped out by lava the tradition was it had to be built again, as soon as it was possible, but in red brick. At Cantoniere di Etna I was taken to see a houseful of catacomb figures in their funeral finery of a century ago. They had been bought at auction, and were now kept not only as a curiosity but because their presence, mysteriously enough, 'helped to steady the nerves'. Two miles up the road the great mountain had spawned a series of small pyramids as if in a self-imitation, and these appeared and vanished in the tides of mist.

I found a room for the night at Zafferana, dashing off next morning in a disorganized and planless fashion, enchanted by the weirdness of this landscape slanting

up to the sky and determined to see as much of it as
I could. People cut off from normal human routine in
such places are inevitably at risk from the mania that can,
for example, fill a living room with catacomb figures.
Nature is constantly surprising in such a setting. Earth
and sky tilt, rain hisses on scalding rocks, a path leading
nowhere is barred by a cast-iron queen (or goddess)
holding a rusted sword. Grape-vines gone wild climb
through a wood full of blue violets. There are shrunken,
discoloured fields of snow and even great rocks perched
among the tundra.

Spurts of rain kept on falling out of a blue sky. There
were great beds of yellow daisies all around and they
gave off a tremendous smell as the water splashed on
their petals. A St Agatha in a black shrine and a garlanded
goddess accompanied each other in the square below the
town hall. A charming little church was surrounded by
groups of shepherds with sun-blackened faces who held
newborn lambs in their sleeves. Woods grew in ravines
full of blue flowers leading to the summit of the volcano.
One of the shepherds, who seemed to be proud of the
eruption, came over to tell me that the lava flow was
moving at nine miles a day. This was certainly a queer
part of the world.

The villagers' approach to the lava flow (moving in
fact at this point at only ten feet a day) was a respectful
one, and a man of obvious authority ordered them to
stand well back. Bulldozers were working all night
to deflect the flow and to cut a new road releasing
those stranded by the eruption. A rescue by jeep varied
in cost between 18,000 and 22,000 lire – say £10 at
most. In the morning a bulldozer took me and the
motorbike five miles up a steep slope covered with

people collecting coloured stones spawned up overnight from the bowels of the earth. Bulldozers were struggling up like tanks in an attack, their drivers shouting with laughter. Little pyramids of lava, some only a few feet high, had sprouted here and there and the chemicals blasted out of the crater were turning them green. Where any vegetation had been left by the fire it gave off a smell of cooking vegetables. Outside Milo I unloaded the motorbike and went riding off over a good road to the north. Linguaglossa was bad again. Rivers of lava were spreading down through the vineyards. At this point I suddenly remembered a section member who was on detachment there and I found him through the police. His name was Potts, although he could have passed as an Italian.

'What's it like here?' I asked him.

'Indescribably boring,' he said. 'All the girls go to Mass on Sunday evenings, and then keep out of the way.'

'Any bandits?'

'There used to be a few, but they call themselves Separatists now. It's going to give the army the chance to wipe them out. We had a late frost in the spring so the wine won't be worth drinking this year.'

We happened at that moment to be standing at the entrance to the town under a banner stretched from one side of the road to the other. UNDER THE VOLCANO YOU COME CLOSEST OF ALL TO SICILY, it said. Potts shook his head. 'I offered the clerk of the Council a few thousand lire to take that down,' he said, 'but there was nothing doing. Who wanted to be under a volcano anyway, and for Christ's sake we were close enough to Sicily at any time as it was.'

3

AFTER THAT BRIEF wartime visit, in the 1950s I returned to Sicily on several occasions to write articles for the *New Yorker* and the *Sunday Times*. These led eventually to the completion of a book, *The Honoured Society*, on that enigmatic island. In researching *The Honoured Society*, I was assisted by running into James McNeish, who had succeeded in exploring what must have been then the least-known part of Mediterranean Europe, the Cammarata Mountains. He had been sent there by the BBC to record the ancient folk music of the area and one of his first contacts was the local Mafia overlord who rode up to his tent on a white horse, and offered his services in a most engaging manner. All that would be required of James in exchange, he said, would be to change his religion. Although James declined as gracefully as he could, the *mafioso* still proved helpful in a place where it was unlikely that an Englishman had been seen before.

I next joined forces with Marcello Cimino, a senior journalist on the staff of *L'Ora* of Palermo. He arranged a number of explorations of the less well-known areas of the island, and his unrivalled knowledge of Sicilian topography made light of journeys among sparsely inhabited mountains, and along coasts that could only be reached on foot. We made our first journey in 1961, and by little more than good luck had soon seen so much of a world that had only just slipped quietly out of the dark ages, that the idea grew of dedicating a month or two in the coming years to further travels and then settling down together to write a book.

These journeys, undertaken in an ancient Fiat, often took us into areas drained of people during the war-time years. Many young men had disappeared, lost to sight for ever in the Western Desert of North Africa. Mussolini had temporarily suppressed the *mafiosi*, but now that his reign was over they were at the point of recovering their strength. Bandits had taken control in many remote areas, and at nightfall mountain villages barricaded themselves in against desperate men sometimes near to starvation. Marcello explained that they worked for food when they could, on isolated hill farms, and turned into bandits at night. Most of them were boys in their teens, and when the police caught them they would deal with them by crushing their toes. In these remote parts Sicily was a place of emptiness, of desolation and elusive beauty and, stopping the car, we would hear only the clicking of insects or sometimes the distant braying of an ass that had returned to the wild.

On the first of our explorations together, Marcello suggested a pilgrimage to Piana degli Albanesi, a small town some sixteen miles south of Palermo. In so far as

Sicily attracted tourists in those days, they were invariably taken to Piana. Its people were descended from Albanian refugees whom the Italians had allowed to settle there, and they had retained their old mode of dress and a number of picturesque customs which had induced both King Victor Emmanuel and Mussolini to pay them visits. Both these occasions produced unsatisfactory results: the King was tricked into adopting one of the local children, while Mussolini, discovering that the mayor was a secret *mafioso*, clapped him in gaol.

Piana came into view against a backdrop of mountains, squeezed among rocky outcrops wherever space could be found. For a short time a single, pale upthrust of rock, curved like a tusk, hid the lake, which appeared less like a body of water than an immense crystal afloat upon a cushion of air. The mayor, stiff as a hussar on parade, awaited us outside the *municipio* with a short list of the town's attractions. A little behind and to one side a young lady presented herself in a silk gown of the old style embroidered in silver and gold thread. Her sleeves sparkled with coloured glass and she wore a hat shaped like a helmet with gold coins dangling on her forehead. A fragrance of incense reached us from the nearby church door and with it came the thin oriental wailing of a choir. The mayor shook our hands. 'Please consider yourselves honorary citizens of this town,' he said.

Our conversation, as was to be expected, was chiefly on the subject of Piana's urgent need to benefit from the growing tourist market. With a nod in the direction of the splendidly attired young woman, the mayor complained of the community's dependence on the past. 'We are the victims of folklore,' he said, 'which does little to fill empty stomachs. Our girls spend their lives making beautiful clothes which they wear only once a year for the Easter processions. In our churches we sing the old hymns using words that many of our youngsters do not understand. The church walls are covered with ikons of our own making, but no one will buy them in the shops. Well, gentlemen, the fact is we have a right to live, too.'

'They tell me you have guided tours of your wonderful caves,' said Marcello.

'The first time round a tourist was lost for four hours, and we abandoned the project. In any case you look at a cave once, and you go away. Signor Cimino, people do not stay here because there is no hotel. If they are hungry, there is nowhere to eat. A bus goes to Palermo twice a week. The children walk four miles to Altofonte to school. Art and history are all very well, but we're isolated. If we don't do something soon even the children will go away.'

'What's the remedy?' Marcello asked. 'Have you anything in mind?'

'Yes,' the mayor said. 'We have lived long in the past, and now we shall look to the future.'

He led the way down through a narrow passage and we came out on a ledge above the lake. This was so clear that we could see the rocks on its bottom, and small green birds were twittering everywhere at its edge. After the old town's undecipherable smells, the air here was suddenly clean and sweet. 'In this lake lies the Albanian people's future,' said the mayor. 'Piana is to become a centre of sport. This is our decision.'

'It will bring about enormous changes,' I told him.

'Yes,' he said. 'From being poor we shall be rich.'

'What kind of sport had you in mind?' Marcello asked him.

'Every kind,' the mayor said. 'All varieties of what we call *turismo lacustre*, including scuba-diving, water-skiing and spear fishing, for which we shall introduce the right species, one which can be easily caught. A children's beach will possess its own swimming pool. There will be a fauno-floristic reserve and a landing stage to cope with vessels of all sizes as well as a properly equipped centre for repairs. The resort in itself will employ hundreds of persons and up to a thousand visitors from northern Europe are expected in the first year. An application has been made for our town to change its name to Piana del Lago, and we believe that this will be granted.'

'Where are the hotels to be built?' Marcello asked.

'A convention will grant building rights on the whole surrounding area,' the mayor said.

'And how soon is all this going to happen?'

The mayor's gesture spoke of the conflict between optimism and doubt. He shook his head.

'I'll come and see you for the Easter procession next year,' Marcello told him.

On the drive back to Palermo the talk was of the Portella massacre of 1947 and of its extraordinary place in the history of Sicily. On the morning of 1 May, less than two weeks after Sicily's impoverished peasants had voted for land reform, villagers from Piana were gunned down during their May Day celebrations at Portella della Ginestra. The massacre had been organized by right-wing politicians in league with the last of the island's outlaw bands in order to stop the peasants from occupying uncultivated land, as they were entitled to do by a law recently passed by the newly elected Sicilian Regional Parliament.

Marcello explained that the elections had in reality been a contest between the Christian Democrats – the party of the landowners, the Church and the Mafia – and a Popular Front amalgam of the parties of the Left. To general surprise, and despite the best efforts of the Church and the Mafia, the Left – champions of the repressed, semi-feudal peasantry – carried the day. Describing the tactics employed in canvassing, Marcello cited the efforts of the Sisters in the small town of Petralia, who visited every house with presents of food and thousand-lire notes for those who would promise to vote for the party of the Church. Those who failed to do so were threatened with losing what land they had. Although Piana possessed no Communist party, after the Left won the election the Right decided to use them as an example to the recalcitrant peasantry in general.

To carry out the task they chose the bandit Salvatore Giuliano, leader of the last remaining wartime band. This brilliant young outlaw had enlisted his followers at the age of sixteen, and had then been bold enough to present himself at the offices of *L'Ora* and provide a lengthy and self-congratulatory interview. His speciality was kidnapping and his victims were often aristocrats like Count Tasca, who was held for a few weeks in a mountain cave and later spoke of Giuliano's charm and excellent manners. Tasca spent much of his time writing poetry and when Giuliano asked him to read a few passages, the bandit praised the result and even suggested a few small alterations.

This was the man, said Marcello, who had been chosen to teach a lesson to the alleged reds at Piana. It was clear that Giuliano himself truly believed that the humble villagers had become communists.

The peasants had been ready before dawn with their preparations for the May Day fiesta, and with the rising of the sun a long procession of painted carts carried them to Portella – the open space under the Pizzuta mountain where the celebrations had always been held. As the procession set off, Giuliano's bandits were taking up their positions on the flanks of the mountain facing the fairground below. It is believed that they were carrying the latest American arms, corroborating evidence being a letter from Giuliano to a U.S. Army Lieutenant Stern which fell into police hands. In it Giuliano insisted that he must have heavier weapons, including mortars and artillery. Later, eight hundred empty cartridge cases were found strewn around an American machine-gun on the mountainside. Three boys reported seeing bandits in U.S. Army uniforms leave the scene.

The number of casualties suffered by the peasants in the ensuing massacre was given as sixty-six, but neither this nor any other figure relating to the episode need necessarily be believed since all the information released passed through a sieve of frequently absurd lies. The true facts about the massacre at Portella instantly became one of the Italian State secrets of the century, for of 2,012 documents relating to the massacre in the possession of the Anti-Mafia Commission all but forty-one have continued to remain secret. In an account of these transactions written for *L'Ora*, Marcello Cimino reported, 'Senator Pafundo, who was for some time president of the Parliamentary Commission of Inquiry, said that the archives contained material that would cause a national catastrophe if they ever came to light.'

Once Giuliano's mission had been completed, the only remaining problem for the secret men who had given him his orders was to rid the country of the bandit and his men with the minimum of publicity and with all possible speed. Most of the rank-and-file bandits were rapidly caught and disposed of, several being added to the scrupulously kept list of those – now amounting to over five hundred names – who had slipped on the stairs at the Ucciardone prison. With the exception of Pisciotta, his cousin and originally his second-in-command, Giuliano was now alone. A secret deal was arranged whereby both men would be allowed to leave Sicily and fly to the U.S.A. in a military plane. Sicily, however, where such deals are endlessly arranged, will always be Sicily, and betrayals are the normal thing. While he was waiting for the plane the Mafia arranged for Giuliano to stay in Castelvetrano, in the house of one De Maria, a low-level *mafioso* lawyer suffering from religious mania, who would later tell the press, 'Our conversations were of faith, good and evil, and redemption. He once told me that he was sure that had fate brought our paths together earlier in his life, his destiny would have been a very different one.' De Maria added that Giuliano spent much of his time reading Shakespeare and Descartes. Six months later a warrant was issued against this God-fearing man for complicity with banditry and participation in an armed band.

Pisciotta, now in the power of the police, left his leader for a day or two. Returning, he found Giuliano asleep in bed and shot him dead. The three carabinieri who were next on the scene decided that it should be made to look as though the bandit had died in combat, so Giuliano's body was dragged downstairs and pitched face down in the courtyard. There the carabinieri captain fired two bursts into it from his sub-machine-gun. Insufficient blood issued from these wounds so one of De Maria's chickens was snatched from its coop and decapitated. In the morning Guiliano's mother and sister were led into the mortuary to identify the body. That task completed, the old lady asked to be taken to the courtyard of De Maria's house, where she knelt down and licked the blood off the flags. Soon the press were on the scene, and for those photographers who arrived late – the Giuliano family having by now been taken back to their home in Montelepre – a black-shrouded crone of local origin was kept in readiness to re-enact the frantic scene.

This trivial but ugly imposture set the mood for the day. The hundreds of excited but frustrated journalists who filled the streets of Castelvetrano pieced together what rumours they could uncover and joined in an orgy of imaginative reconstruction of the events of the previous night. The evening editions of the Italian papers carried detailed accounts, sometimes almost shot by shot, of street battles in which – according to the *Gazzetta del Popolo* – 350 carabinieri were involved. A fog of lies had been released like a genie from its bottle, and it was months before the genie could be squeezed back in and the cork rammed home.

The elimination of Giuliano had been arranged by the State, yet Pisciotta was now charged with murder and he was held in the Ucciardone prison between sessions of the court during his trial. It had become clear that he shared in the deadly secrets for which

Giuliano had been removed from the scene, and there is little doubt that discussions took place as how best to impose the 'essential silence' in his case. When Pisciotta, who clearly feared for his life, had been in prison before, he had surprisingly enough been able to keep with him a caged bird on which he tested his food. This was ruled out at the Ucciardone – a veto which had the effect of increasing his precautions when food of any kind was placed before him. But he suffered from a chest complaint, and a doctor in whom he placed some reliance prescribed a vitamin concentrate to be added to whatever food he felt able to eat. However, after the first dose of this he was taken ill and he passed away later the same day.

The true facts about the massacre at Portella remained concealed for fifty years. Then, in 1997, the Anti-Mafia Commission announced that the secret documents concerning the massacre were at last to be published. These were known to contain proofs of the undemocratic combination of landlords, the Mafia and the Church to prevent the peasants taking over uncultivated land, and there were further documents dealing with the instigators of the bandits' attack in May 1947, and the supposed supply to them of U.S. Army weapons. From year to year it had been promised that these documents would be produced for public scrutiny, but the moment passed, silence fell and matters of trivial local interest once again occupied the stage.

A few years later a letter of protest from the father of a local policeman killed by the Mafia, addressed to the President of the Republic, was published. 'In 1989,' said the writer, 'my son, daughter-in-law and their children were wiped out by the Mafia. I note that it has taken fifty years for us to be told anything about the Portella massacre. Does that mean that I, an old man, must look forward to a forty-year delay before I find out what happened to my dear ones – who killed them and why?'

Possibly this letter had some effect, for in July 1999 a spokesman for the government assured the Italian people that an investigation into the massacre was to be opened after all, and that the Anti-Mafia Commission would reveal the contents of the documents that had so successfully guarded their secrets until now. They were to be passed over for scrutiny by lawyers appointed by the families involved. Amazingly, the Ministry of the Interior now conceded the general view that the massacre at Portella was 'one of the most obscure moments of our history, which has contributed to the hindrance and delay in the affirmation of democracy and legality in our country'.

After the massacre, as tensions gradually began to ease, the government turned its attentions to the future prospects and morale of the rural population. Marcello's first major undertaking after joining *L'Ora* was to test the attitudes of the agrarian population, and in particular the degree of confidence they felt in the advertised advantages promised them by the new laws.

The results were negative in the extreme. Some peasants took the view that the Portella massacre was a forerunner of others to come, and the promised redistribution of uncultivated land would lead to little but disappointment. From the beginning huge delays were clearly to be involved in putting such reforms into practice. It eventually took fifteen years to distribute uncultivated land on the Nelson estate at Bronte, for instance, and it turned out here and elsewhere that a grant of fifteen acres, the maximum to which each peasant was entitled, was too small to support a family. The government's much boosted Anti-Mafia Commission was described by Marcello's informants as a political diversion and a waste of time. He himself noted that the Sicilian peasantry had lost their capacity for hope. Between 1951 and 1953, 400,000 Sicilians – more than 10 per cent of the population – had emigrated. The majority were working males, and in some areas only old people, women and children were left behind to work the fields. Even before Marcello began his investigation, 20 per cent of the feudal estates found themselves without labour.

With the most effective members of its peasant class lost to emigration, a drastic increase of poverty took place in Sicily. In 1959, Professor Silvio Pampiglione of the University of Rome, who was to become a friend of Marcello's, carried out a project based upon Palma di Montechiaro, a town somewhat larger than Piana degli Albanesi, although otherwise facing similar disadvantages.

Pampiglione investigated the lives of 600 families, producing a report said at the time to have shocked the Italian conscience, although it had little effect on the conditions the professor described. The 600 families, he found, occupied 700 rooms – 4.86 persons to a room – 216 of which possessed no window. Such habitations are known as *bassi*, and still exist all over the remoter parts of Sicily as well as on the outskirts of Palermo. Basically a single door provides the influx of air, although in other cases an opening in the wall not always covered by glass may pass as a window. Only fifty-two of the houses studied in this case possessed a water supply, and eighty-two a lavatory, which in some cases was no more than a hole in the corner of a room.

Shortages of living space involved other problems. Every family was compelled to supplement its income by keeping a variety of animals, and as there were no pens or outhouses where these valuable possessions could be kept in safety they had to be brought in to sleep with the family at night. Thus sharing 700 rooms with 3,404 humans were 5,085 animals, including goats, pigs, donkeys, horses and mules. On one occasion the professor was hospitably offered a glass of goat's milk. 'Where does the goat sleep at night?' he asked, and was told, 'Under the bed.' 'But doesn't the stink kill you?' 'You get used to it, like everything else, in time.' The implications for hygiene were clearly catastrophic. There were ten bakeries in the area covered by the professor's investigations, and in every case the family's animals were lodged in the bakery. In one case the dough was prepared and the loaves finally produced in a cavern sheltering three humans, a donkey, a mule, four goats and twelve hens.

Poverty at this level inevitably adds to the crime figures. In the first place it shows in the increase of the low-level depredations of sneak thieves who steal hens from the coops, and this adds to the misery of the poor. The more efficient members of this criminal small-fry find eventual promotion into the local underworld, until a break-in or the theft of a car attracts the attention of a *mafioso* enlisting *picciotti* (small-time criminals) to help him in more serious levels of crime. Such a *picciotto* (said to have been trembling with terror) killed my friend Boris Giuliano of the Pubblica Sicurezza years later in 1979, shooting him with six bullets in the back while he sipped his morning coffee at the counter of the Bar Lux, Palermo.

In the wake of the mass emigration of the 1950s all forms of Mafia-inspired criminality were to increase. Sicily is full of tragic records. After Calabria it has always been the most impoverished area in Italy, and comes close to being the worst in Europe. In the grim anarchy of the post-war years, when even the owners of minor feudal estates decided on emigration, killers went to work for a fixed rate of 200,000 lire (£130) per corpse. As the heads of the various Mafia families fought each other over the declining spoils, the homicide rate in Palermo rose to become the highest in the world apart from the small town of Favara. This had suffered 130 Mafia killings in a single year and the Duce in his time had been told that only one man in the previous decade had died of natural causes.

4

FOR ONE REASON or another, despite a promising start, the idea that Marcello and I would write a book together had to be postponed. His obligations to his newspaper were too many. I therefore returned to England shortly after our first excursion, but was almost immediately engaged by the *Sunday Times* to cover a sensational Mafia trial to be staged in Palermo, which by chance happened to provide a postscript to my memories of the Portella business. The trial had aroused considerable interest internationally since it was the first time that criminal cooperation had been proved between the leading Sicilian *mafiosi* and American members of Cosa Nostra. For the first time 'men of respect' from both sides of the Atlantic were to stand trial together.

Marcello came to my aid in this undertaking and was able to borrow *L'Ora*'s photographer, a Signor Lo Buono, who had exceptional access to all such events, and place him at my disposition. He told me with a laugh that Lo Buono was a low-grade man of respect.

'As a photographer he's nothing special,' he said. 'What matters is he knows how to handle the judge.'

The trial would provide us with a splendid opportunity to get together again and perhaps even to finish the book. We made arrangements over the phone as Marcello was away in Catania at that moment. He thought that the trial would occupy some time, although he hoped to return within the week, after which he would twist *L'Ora*'s arm into giving him substantial leave of absence and we could get down to work. He sounded a little less ebullient than usual on this occasion, but I put this down to the poor connection.

Lo Buono turned out to be small, impish and full of good cheer, and whatever his supposed standing in the Honoured Society he was a man it would have been hard to dislike. We passed through the line of carabinieri guarding the door of the courthouse as if they had not been there. An usher awaited us just inside. He bowed slightly. 'Signor Lo Buono,' he said, 'will you be taking photographs today?' Smiling pleasantly, Lo Buono replied, 'I expect to do that.' It was a hot day outside and the street was full of noise, but the court was as cool and calm as a church. It had the faint odour of hassocks so often to be detected in a very large interior that is rarely used.

The judge had already taken his seat beneath a notice saying that photography was strictly forbidden. Lo Buono levelled his camera, focused and took a shot, and the judge nodded his head in our direction in acquiescence if not in gratitude. With that a door opened in the rear wall and the prisoners filed in and took their seats in the dock. By all accounts they had spent a year or so in the notoriously gloomy environment of the Ucciardone, yet all these men in their summer suits sported notable suntans. It was later to transpire that they were not only American versions of men of respect, but men of substance, too. Evidence had been produced in court that back in the States they had close associations with leading personalities of the Catholic Church, who had spoken on their behalf. Two had sons training for the priesthood, and one had actually built and paid for an orphanage. This was to be their last but one appearance in court before the trial came to an end with the clearance of all defendants for lack of proof, and their release.

Lo Buono packed his lenses away and we went out into the street. It occurred to me that although I had been on a number of occasions in the company of men rumoured to be *mafiosi*, this was my first experience of being with one positively identified as such by a newspaperman of the kind that did not exaggerate. He seemed pleased when I suggested a coffee and we crossed the road and settled in a café. There had been an extraordinary scene in court when the prisoners' wives and children had been led in by the carabinieri to stand in a row under the front of the dock. With this the prisoners were released from the long chain to which they were fastened, allowing them to pass down to wives and children the presents they had brought with them.

This came up in the café. 'So that's one you couldn't take,' I said. 'Do you mean the carabinieri wouldn't stand for it?'

'I have an arrangement with the carabinieri. They eat out of my hand.'

'What was the problem, then?'

'The women,' he said. 'The wives. I can't take that

kind of picture. When there's a woman in the picture I have to ask myself do I take it or don't I? In this case the answer was no. I work for *L'Ora*. You probably heard that its office was bombed a couple of years back. They play things carefully these days.'

He changed the subject. 'Your friend said you were here before. What were you doing?'

'I was writing about Giuliano.'

'You ought to talk to his brother.'

'I didn't know he had one. Not a bandit, is he?'

'No, he's up at the service station. Enrico works on the pumps. We pass the place on the way to your hotel. Might interest you to see him.'

'It would,' I said. 'Can I use the story?'

'I'll tell you if you can't.'

Enrico was on the forecourt polishing a windscreen and Lo Buono called him over. 'This is Salva's brother,' Lo Buono said, and for a moment I believed there had been some mistake. Even the worst of the many photographs taken of Giuliano could not have extinguished the fire and the laughter in his face. How could Enrico, limping towards us, eyes screwed up in perplexity and rag in hand, be of the same blood? It was twenty years since Pisciotta's bullets had blasted away Giuliano's heart, but surely the slow leakage of time had not been long enough to turn the brother of that heroic savage into this emblem of defeat. Enrico drooped before us, wincing a nervous smile. 'Friend from England to see you,' Lo Buono said, and Enrico dropped the rag to wipe his hands on his denims and we shook hands.

'First of all, Enrico, what's the news of the job? Are they doing what they said for you?' Lo Buono asked.

'Not so far, Signor Lo Buono. They're going to give Donata a couple of hours a day office-cleaning. It's better than nothing. Her mother will look after the boy.'

'It's not enough,' Lo Buono said. 'I'll have to talk to them again. In the meanwhile I was telling Signor Luigi about you and Salva. Did you see much of each other in the old days at Montelepre?'

'When I was a boy, of course, Signor Lo Buono. You have to remember I was only a kid. He used to look after us, my mother and me.'

'What did he do for a living? Is it true that he was in the black market?'

Still twisting at the rag, Enrico drew his lips back in a drab laugh. 'I never heard of that,' he said. 'He used to trap rabbits for a living. We ate the rabbits and people bought the skins to make coats.'

'But he *was* a bandit, wasn't he?'

'They say so. I was too young to know much about these things. He used to take me to Partinico to sell the rabbit skins. We went to Trappeto once. That's by the sea. I collected a bagful of sea shells. In Montelepre we children used to play with them.'

'Wasn't Salva with the bandits at Portella?'

'No, he was never there. The police wanted him to go but he refused. They offered him three million lire, and told him he'd be arrested and charged with murder if he refused to do what he was told. All Salva would agree to do was to persuade a cousin on our mother's side who looked like him to take over the job. He was called Ludovico and he had one leg shorter than the other. The idea was to tell the others he'd hurt his knee. His chin was different too

31

so he was told to wrap a scarf round the bottom of his face.'

'You're telling me that the bandits didn't know the difference?' Lo Buono said.

'The old ones were in the know. They were supposed to get half a million each. This was the first time the new boys had been used on a thing like this. They'd never set eyes on Salvatore himself. They wouldn't have known him.'

'All this is news to me,' Lo Buono said. 'I've never heard of a cousin. What happened to him?'

'He disappeared.'

'But he was at Portella?'

'He was there. He fired a machine-gun. When it was over the police told them where to go and hide out. I heard that they never saw him again.'

'He just vanished?'

'Off the face of the earth.'

'Enrico,' Lo Buono said, 'it could be as you say, but in my job I can't afford to believe anything, and I don't believe in Ludovico. What I'm thinking now is maybe you have a poor sort of job, but in the end things can only get better for you. Would you have changed places with Salva? The best time either of you ever had was when you were shooting rabbits.'

We walked away, leaving Enrico to his polishing. 'I ought to be angry with him for giving us that story,' Lo Buono said. 'His troubles are driving him mad.'

5

EARLY AUTUMN WITH the Sicilian summer finally in
retreat was the time to travel to Palermo. It was quiet
everywhere, in the streets and shops, and in the offices
of *L'Ora* where sales of the newspaper dropped by
half, with readers still too drugged with the pleasures
of departing summer to bother to check on the market
price of sulphur or face the daily stories of political
skulduggery. Consequently, on 7 September 1990 the
taxi from Punta Raisi Airport dropped me at Marcello's
home, 110 Via Maqueda, and once again I climbed the
staircase wandering through the lower parts of this
ancient building, arriving finally at the top-flat rooms
and roof garden where I knew that my friends would
be waiting. They were there, as I had seen them so
often before, each in his or her favourite place in sun
or in shade. It was one of those environments that
suppressed evidence of change. There were the little
trees in their pots, the trellis drooping its honeysuckle
among the tiny blue butterflies, the swifts that came
screeching out of the sky to snatch up an insect fluttering

within feet of one's face. Hundreds of feet below, the endless procession of traffic droned softly up and down the Via Maqueda. My friends took me in their embrace: Marcello and his wife Giuliana, who was an authoress and politician, her sister Gabriella, a stage designer, and a young man I saw here for the first time, Gioacchino Lavanco, who worked with Marcello on *L'Ora* half the week, and spent the other half lecturing on politics at the university.

Marcello announced that he had just returned from the family's vineyard. The harvest, he said, had been the best for years. 'The rain came at the right time. It makes all the difference,' he told me.

'How many bottles?' I asked.

'Fewer than usual. About three hundred. But that's the trouble with the good smaller grapes, you have to expect it. Still it's worth it. We're quite happy.'

At some time during an exchange of views that followed on the topic of viniculture I began to experience a curious sensation. Gabriella's head was always full of inventions, and her thoughts, affected – as to be expected – by the surrealistic nature of her work, flew like birds from one subject to the next. But today she seemed strangely distracted and detached from what was going on. Marcello's mouth close to my ear said, 'I managed to pick up an old map of the Aiutamicristo the other day. I'd like to show it to you.'

We crossed the roof to a lumber room where he kept a few pictures and books. 'What do you think of Gioacchino?' he asked.

'He's very likeable. Clever, too, I suspect.'

'They think a lot of him at the office. I ask you because there's some bad news. I have to go into hospital on Tuesday, which means I can't come with you after all. Sorry I couldn't let you know sooner.'

'My God. What on earth's the trouble?'

'There's no reason I shouldn't tell you. It's cancer. I spoke to Gioacchino yesterday and he's offered to take my place. You'd never find a more knowledgeable or pleasant companion.'

'Does Giuliana know about it?'

'They all know. It's the liver. At the moment there's no pain. Only numbness. When were you planning to leave?'

'I hadn't any plans, not knowing what you had in mind. The last thing I want to do is to bother you at a time like this. Poor Giuliana. What on earth will she do?'

'I'd very much like not to disappoint Gioacchino,' Marcello said. 'This little bother will take its time. My suggestion is to leave things at the moment as they are. If you preferred you could make this a short excursion. Go off for a few days and come back. Now here's a suggestion. Gioacchino says there's something important due to happen at Bagheria tomorrow. It's only an hour's drive away and if I can get the doctor and Giuliana to agree I might at least come as far as that with you.' For a second or two his eyes closed, then reopened, and at this moment I realized that this was an encounter with a hero.

Next day the doctor's verdict was that journeys for Marcello, however short, were out of the question. The news was broken by Marcello himself who urged us, via Giuliana, in no circumstances to miss Bagheria and reminded us that he was looking forward to our report.

As regards Bagheria, I remembered a previous visit

to this town and that I had left it with a sensation almost of relief. People, in particular foreign tourists, went there to visit the Villa Palagonia, a strange, eerie building described by the Sicilian lady who had shown me round on a previous visit as giving her the shivers. It had been created two and a half centuries earlier, and the original villa was regarded as an outstanding example of Sicilian baroque architecture. But as the years passed and the third generation of the Gravina family began to exhibit the symptoms – evident in all their undertakings – of mental collapse, a high, encircling wall was built, cutting off most of the view of the villa. This wall was surmounted by a nightmarish collection of grotesque human and animal figures carved in the golden sandstone. The creator of this fantasy appears positively to have admired a brand of ugliness which must have produced nightmares in many a child forced to accompany its parents on a visit to this revolting scene.

What is curious is that an exceptional number of *mafiosi* were known to have settled comfortably in this environment. Eight years after that visit to Bagheria, Bernardo Provenzano, who broke all records as a fugitive from justice, was reported to have spent a high proportion of his thirty years on the run in these surroundings which suited him so well, living in security and great style in a villa within easy view of the Gravina monstrosity.

The local event to which Marcello had referred, and of which through the newspaper he had received information in advance, was concerned with a persistent feud between two *capi-mafia*: Totò Riina – then regarded as the head of Cosa Nostra – and the ferocious Luciano Leggio who had thrust his way to the front years before with his much publicized murder in Corleone of the trade union leader Placido Rizzotto.

It turned out that the war for the possession of Bagheria had already broken out by the time we arrived; all shops were closed, all cars parked, and what Lorca described as a 'stinking silence' had settled over the town. Not a pedestrian was in sight. Gioacchino managed to shove the car away out of view, and as he did so a single carabiniere materialized in a doorway, ready with news. He was unusually communicative and seemed happy to be released from his boring routine. We would be interested, he thought, to hear that Leggio was marshalling his forces somewhere in the neighbourhood, despite the fact that officially he was at that moment incarcerated in the maximum-security prison at Termini Imerese. He was conducting the battle by telephone.

Totó Riina's people had engaged their opponents in a brief machine-gun battle earlier that morning. It was clear that such incidents were almost a matter of routine.

'A lot of machine-gun fire in the morning,' the carabiniere said, 'to start off the day. After that usually nothing to speak of. It always quietens down in the afternoon. My advice is to go to Alcamo. You'll find plenty of activity down there.'

Whatever his personal inclinations, Gioacchino thought he had to follow the man's advice. The carabiniere took us to the station where Gioacchino phoned the *maresciallo* of the carabineri at Alcamo. 'It's fairly exciting,' he said. 'By all means come along.' Somewhat to our surprise he arranged to meet us not at carabinieri headquarters, but at a spot on the outskirts of the town.

Alcamo, a fine white town overflowing with magnificent churches, is heaped over the top of a hill with the most elegant parts of it, as is usual in such cases, on display at the summit. The rendezvous was to be at the end of a path down to the main road, and a dark-haired girl of about twenty was awaiting us, her dramatic facial expression I suspected, whatever the circumstances, of being unvarying. This was the *maresciallo*'s daughter and her news was that he and his five carabinieri were under siege by Totò Riina's men, and at that moment no one could enter or leave the town. There was nothing for it but to turn back. It was an incident that for me showed the Mafia mentality in a new light. Women were always employed as messengers at such moments of tension, Gioacchino explained, both by the Mafia and the police, and their neutrality respected. 'Working for the newspaper, you see these things happen all the time,' he said. '*Mafioso* wives and lovers do most of the negotiating that goes on with the police, or maybe the *maresciallo*'s daughter is invited to sit down for a comfortable chat with the superboss, and is charmed by the old-fashioned courtesy she is shown.

'Pity you won't be here for the Festa della Morte,' he went on.

'Anything like Mexico?' I asked.

'Nothing,' Gioacchino said. 'It's part of a child's upbringing. They're brought up here not to fear death. The kids are pushed out into the street and fed cake. The very young ones get sugar dolls.'

'Not so very different from a child's treat anywhere else,' I suggested.

'It is,' Gioacchino said. 'The Devil brings the presents. If it's a really poor family it could be the only present he or she ever gets. Anyway it's something to remember. The parents and the Devil go through a series of gestures to indicate that they're passing on the fear of death to the rich.'

There was an autostrada to be crossed when we left police headquarters. Gioacchino warned us that there was no underpass so we would have to wait or take our chances. 'A few days ago they found the body of a man who'd been hit by a car with the sugar doll from his childhood still in his pocket,' Gioacchino told me.

I was making notes. 'Any more?' I asked.

Gioacchino said, 'Yes. There is no word for pleasure in the local dialect.'

There was a restaurant just down the road of the kind that opens only at weekends, and we went in to sit for a while over a bottle of wine and decide what to do next. The owner served us with the local pasta full of small sea shells. 'Notice anything unusual?' Gioacchino asked, and I shook my head.

'He has two thumbs on his right hand, which is good for business. People will pay a bit more here just to see the thumbs. They're very fond of unusual things – well, in a way. They took a great dislike to the telephone kiosks and used to stone them when they were first put in. The police had *Ti Amo* (I love you) painted on all the boxes, and after that they let them alone. All prostitutes are small. Now why should that be? The best-looking ones ask to be paid in cocaine. The beggars pay the Mafia for their positions outside the churches. They have to wear a kind of uniform with patches sewn into it, but for beggars they're rich. If they finally let us in the town we must go to the office of the tourist agency. The lady who runs it half opens the door and then stands sideways while she's talking to you so as to show only half her figure,' Gioacchino said. 'These people try to convince themselves they're townsfolk, but actually they're living the life of villagers – maybe of a few hundred years ago.'

Gioacchino's stories of the surrounding Mafia strongholds had filled half my notebook, each one in some way different from the rest, but all with a reputation for toughness and crime. 'Why don't we take a look at Corleone after all?' Gioacchino said. 'I have an idea you'll find it changed since you last went there.'

We were already in the outskirts of this celebrated town and he nodded in the direction of a splendid façade in pale sandstone soaring above a rank of parked cars. 'La Chiesa Madre. Magnificent, isn't it?'

'And well looked-after,' I said.

'They can afford to,' Gioacchino said. 'Plenty of money about, and the Church gets its share.'

'Someone told me this place is pretty run down these days?'

'Maybe it was, but no longer. They're into cocaine now, and business for everybody is good. Those aren't just pigeons you see up there,' he said. 'They're turtle doves of some special kind from the Holy Land. A present from the cardinal. Drugs are the best money-spinner these days.'

Our road back to Palermo was as straight as we could make it, through villages such as Marineo and Bolognetta where 'respected' families forbade their daughters to show themselves on balconies even when the usual sheeting had been stretched behind the rails to conceal the lower parts of their bodies. The very old in such towns were laid outside the house daily in a drying process which they believed diminished the pangs of death.

At the entrance to Palermo there'd been a crash. There were tiny brilliant puddles of blood under the cars. A calm discussion was going on between the survivors, and passers-by brought sweets for the children.

The news of Marcello was worse. He had been obliged to take to his bed, but despite his realization that the end must be near there was no change in his humour or spirit – even a wry little touch of self-congratulation again in the matter of the grape harvest. Marcello died a week later, and for me, it was like the loss of a family member.

Changing plans, I decided to do no more than fulfil my contract with the *Sunday Times* and to postpone major literary effort involving the island to some future time, which as it transpired meant a delay of eight years.

6

IN 1998, CORRESPONDING with my Sicilian friends in preparation for a renewed visit, I was assured by them that I should find everything much changed. I assumed at first that this would be for the better, but alighting from the taxi at a modest hotel some yards from the Quattro Canti, Palermo, at about eleven at night I was not wholly sure that this was the case.

Palermo's historic centre has always been patrician and austere, but now it was also silent. My wife, Lesley, and I asked at the hotel reception desk whether we could get something to eat, but our request was met by shaken heads.

All the staff had gone home. Eventually we were despatched in search of a nearby trattoria thought possibly to be open. There were neither pedestrians nor vehicles of any kind in sight. Pale lamps illuminated the street and the ranks of tall, stark buildings, their summits sunk in the blue-black sky. Most of the windows were shuttered and all the doors closed. The only movement was the flinch in the shadows of a cat mobilized by night. The owner of the trattoria stood at the back of twenty empty tables to welcome us with a tight half-smile. He was grateful for our unexpected presence in this place where the glitter of barren place-settings deepened the solitude. He made us an omelette and, as we were leaving, came to the door to squeeze my hand and turn out all but one of the lights. 'If you are approached,' he said to me in an undertone, 'allow your hands to fall to your sides.'

We went out into the street which, in its emptiness, glistened strangely as if the surface had been oiled. We were making our way quickly back to the hotel when we heard a low growling sound in the distance. This increased, for a moment to a point when the earth seemed to vibrate, and I suspected a tremor of the kind I had had some experience of in the south of mainland Italy. Then a machine turned a bend in the road ahead. At first it looked like a gigantic earth-mover supporting a tower with a small platform at its top. Several men dressed in protective clothing were busy with machinery, and when the thing came to a standstill just ahead of us it shot out a kind of gangway. It became clear that work was to begin on the repair of a palazzo which had recently showered the street below with a small landslide of decorative masonry.

The drama of the coming of dawn in Palermo was exaggerated by the long night's prelude of silence and torpor. Daylight filled the streets with a tempest of sound and clamorous action. The city's huge daily problem within an hour or two of the rising of the sun is the painstaking separation of the mosaic of cars inserted with such patience and skill into hundreds of streets; thereafter the steady if frenetic flow of the traffic recommences. With the approach of nightfall the procedure goes into reverse. Sicilian human society, for all one's presuppositions, displays cooperation, tolerance and good nature. Piece by piece – each fitting exactly in place – the mosaic is reassembled. The blast of car-horns fades away, the roaring exhausts are silenced, the elaborate patterns of parked cars are restored, and what on first acquaintance is the deep calm of the Palermo night returns again.

Spiritually and physically this city is imbued with the classic life of the Mediterranean deep south, and as such is companionable and exuberant, as well as vociferous. To see the best of this, there is no better way than to make for the old part of the town. In our case, with a base at the Quattro Canti, this meant following the main Corso Vittorio Emanuele eastwards for some two hundred yards before turning into any side-street leading to the sea. It was here that a succession of invaders came ashore down the centuries, then settled to build their churches, palaces and forts. It is an experience to broaden the mind, bringing the visitor into immediate contact with human beings who appear to be saturated with the pleasures of Palermo as it once was, rather than the unfortunates who have graduated to the lifelessness and colourlessness of the new suburbs to be reached along the ring roads.

The most interesting street leads through the Vucciria market down to the San Domenico church, and the stalls sloping down to the centre take up two-thirds of the street's width. There can be no more splendid market in the world than this, for the vendors of foodstuffs of every kind are infatuated with extremes of size and artistic presentation. Zucchini are a yard long, but fifty snails can be held in a cupped hand. The tastefully arranged collops of meat are brilliantly and continuously smeared with fresh vermilion blood and the chicken's feet neatly trimmed of their claws. Sideshows attract tiny Sicilian puppets which dance to taped music over traysful of giblets. Bright-eyed cockerels stroll at liberty up and down the street until the moment of execution comes, which may be within seconds of their first appearance.

The area possesses a popular saint of its own, Padre Meli of the parish of Santa Chiara all'Albergheria, esteemed by all for his care of the unfortunate and sick and for his lively tolerance of all religions. 'Let them worship who they will, so long as they worship,' he is supposed to have said, and when the poor Tunisians of the neighbourhood complained that they had no mosque he replied, 'Don't worry, I'll fix one up for you.' And this he did in the cellars under his church.

Humanity is presented here surely in its most concentrated form. In Naples, where I spent the year 1944–45, I noted that the Vicaria district was officially credited with the highest population density in Europe, with three persons occupying every two square metres of floorspace. I am sure that the Vucciria of Palermo could have competed with this with its tightly packed and animated multitudes. There are faces at every window and a bustling, gesticulating crowd at work in every cellar. Apart from the market itself, the area might be seen as a slum, but it is not, for all these people are clean, well dressed, affable and courteous. By night, if possible, there is even greater crowding among the acres of decaying palaces in the city centre. Cars are crammed with extreme skill among the courtyards' chipped and abraded Corinthian columns, while above, girls who for

the best part work in offices sleep twenty or thirty to
a room into which they are packed like tiny inanimate
parcels. There is nothing of the slum about these conditions because morale remains unshaken. From eight
in the morning onwards the young typists and computer operators come, fresh, smart and lively as can be,
streaming out into the streets.

It was estimated in a newspaper report that three hundred of Palermo's splendid palaces – among them superb
examples of baroque architecture – were in desperate
need of repair. Even to the inexpert eye of the casual
passer-by, many of them appeared to have reached
the point of no return and shortly, with or without
warning, the end would be signalled in the thunder of
falling masonry. Such doomed buildings dominate their
environment in many parts of the city. Abandoned
eventually by the nobility, subsequent occupants, drawn
largely from the mercantile class, have been unable to
afford the vast expenditure needed to keep them in
repair, and thus, slowly over the centuries, the processes
of decay have taken their toll. One of the grandest is
the Villa of the Dukes of Pietra Tagliata, residence of
Ferdinand IV after his expulsion from Naples in 1799,
which has just been officially 'sealed', i.e. placed out
of bounds to visitors. 'Of the once majestic façade on
three levels,' says the report, 'little remains. The decorative window and door surrounds and the tessellated
pavements have vanished.' No city could easily afford
the full repair of so many vestiges of a grandiose past,
nor even the cost of rendering them all safe, which
would be high. There they stand, towering over mean
streets, reduced often to façades and outer walls, the
roofs having fallen in. While we were there ten such

palaces were threatened with demolition orders. It is hoped that most will survive for another century or two, for in them Palermo demonstrates the beauty of noble ruin, incomparable even as a purely decorative presence among the mediocrity of the modern equivalents with which they will eventually be replaced.

In theory such palaces have usually been empty for a number of years, with no signs of life visible through the grimy windows of the lower floors, but just as often, almost, curtained windows on the top floors suggest that with or without sanction they are occupied by poorer families, who accept the risk of staying in possession until removed by the police.

During our stay in Palermo, the historic buildings in the last stages of delapidation included the Palace of the Dukes of Acquaviva, a once magnificent, but now abandoned building rumoured to have been converted for use as a pig farm. Government inspectors, visiting it, found that this was indeed a fact. Pigs' excrement covered the floor and that of the palace's adjacent chapel to a considerable depth. Marble floor tiles, and a valuable old wrought-iron balcony railing, had been stolen by thieves who did no more than walk in and carry them off. The legal owner of the edifice was a man of eighty-three, who, despite his legitimate ownership, faced a charge of disfiguring a national monument. He was not impressed, demanding in reply, 'Who was going to look after the dump, if I didn't?'

It was clear that, even with squatters in partial occupation, such buildings were at risk from depredations other than the weather. A case in point was the Palazzo Galletti, a late-baroque palace occupying one side of the Piazza Marina down by the port. In this instance a lady passing by spotted robbers working in full view of the street to remove a marble pillar from one of the decorative windows. Disturbed by the arrival of the police, they made their escape, returning after an hour or two when the coast was quiet to finish their work and carry the pillar away.

Our project for our second day in Palermo was to visit these and several other buildings threatened with closure, but this had to be postponed due to a major dislocation of the city's traffic. A demonstration had been announced by employees of the municipality in protest over wages and working conditions, and a long and slow-moving column of protesters had taken to the streets. Such demonstrations were frequent and their organizers had become masters of the art of imposing total inertia in those parts of the city centre where traffic congestion was at all times an insoluble problem. Experience had taught us that on such occasions excursions could only be undertaken on foot.

In reality this involved no more than a minor change of plans, for in this beehive of human activity many places of great interest within walking distance of the hotel waited to be explored. The pleasant muddle of this great city invites spur-of-the-moment investigation in any direction. Nothing is easier than to make a start up the nearest main street, then branch off into the first side-turning leading inevitably to a great building or a leafy square.

This was clearly the time to step down the nearest alley-way leading to the Ballaro market. We were there in a matter of minutes, plunging into what might have been a corner of Dickensian London. Space is rare in Palermo and wherever it is to be found is put to maximum use. People crammed themselves into cellars at night, and slept on the stair-landings of the old palaces and even in the more capacious cupboards. Recent collapses had provided the Ballaro with a little extra space, now crammed with stalls. All Sicilian towns have their resident magicians, as in the instance of Francesco Gambino of Corleone, in which a substantial minority of the population place their trust. Here small-scale operators were in action with remedies and spells identical in some instances to those employed by the Carthaginians and ancient Greeks, and a whiff of incense cones and burnt offerings came through, mingling comfortably with the special odour of poverty. The sick still swallow down powdered amber, and the dust of St Rita's bones. Where a little space could be claimed a pair of elderly men sat facing each other at small tables playing the card game called *scopo*. On certain feast days, we were told, custom allowed women to gamble in public for small sums of money in this game, although otherwise male and female players are always separated.

The great social reformer Danilo Dolci, whom I had met many years before with James McNeish, mentions that in his time teams involved in the clandestine trade in horse manure roamed the streets at night collecting all they could of this sought-after commodity for use in basement gardens. This was illegal, as the manure was the property of the municipality, and could only be secured on payment of a bribe. Now the last of the thousand or so coaches of the aristocracy are no more and with their loss the trade is at an end.

Hope in such places as this has always been a shallow affair, and visiting the nearby Cortile Cascino back in 1959 Dolci had noted that 498 persons lived in 118 rooms, some 200 yards from the cathedral. Only one family had a lavatory. The others cooked, ate and defecated in their one room, although, as elsewhere, 'decently behaved' males relieved themselves on the railway lines.

Of the city of Palermo it would be fair to say that it is a place of limitless excitements. The newspapers are glutted with sensations. Three leading politicians out of four are generally exposed as corrupt, the death rate by violence is twice that of Rome, a palace falls down every year, State processions are held up by continual funerals, and in 1998 the postal authorities disposed of an accumulation of undelivered letters by burning them or throwing them into the sea. In the poor areas, such as the Albergheria, more people are treated by magicians than by doctors. About one half of the prostitutes are black, of these Nigerians being preferred, 'for the sincerity of their beliefs', and also for their expertise in 'African tricks'. It is generally agreed that the best coffee in the world is served, in semi-slum surroundings, by Tunisian immigrants, who are possessed of huge charm.

Next day – and apparently this was often the case on a Monday – the week's news opened on a note of frivolity. A paper had carried out a detailed investigation into the changing sexual attitudes of the people of Palermo as illustrated by what went on in its famous Parco della Favorita, a pleasure garden extending for a mile or so along the north-western outskirts of the city. This once secluded area, famous until well into this century for the number and frequency of the duels fought there, had also always been seen by the romantically-minded as exceptionally suitable for the conduct of *al fresco* amours. Much as the Sicilians might have adhered to their other customs, in matters sexual the change in attitude as described by newspapermen who surveyed the park with their pocket telescopes was spectacular.

Whatever the encroachment of foreign liberalism, the Sicilians are still inclined by custom to shut away vulnerable females after dark. This is perhaps all to the good if thereby they are assisted in their studies for careers. Nevertheless the new generation was stalwart in its defence of sexual freedoms. The *Giornale della Sicilia* reported that many trysting couples now made for the park in their cars when the sun was still high in the heavens. They were encouraged, the newspaper thought, by the fact that the occupants of so many other cars were clearly there for the same reason. There was one very small drawback. The park authorities had suddenly enlisted uniformed wardens to police the situation, but these were only empowered to impose small fines for damaging the bushes in the course of whatever the cars' occupants were doing.

It was evident even to a visitor like myself that many lovers, unable to find time to drive out to La Favorita, had found substitutes for its leafy environment nearer to home. These included the Via Filangeri, until recently a quiet dead-end down by the port, which had become so crowded that cars were queuing until a parking space became vacant.

Antonio Manganelli, Chief of Police of Palermo, had

written a letter to the press, remarkably liberal in its sentiments. 'I am a broad-minded man,' he said, 'doing my best to move with the times, and I invite my fellow citizens to follow my example. I recommend those who take offence at the sexual antics that have been described simply to look in another direction. Such complaints as have been published are trivial in a city under assault by real criminals, and I refuse to allow my hard-pressed men to be diverted from important duties to attempt to remedy them.'

The hard news that was to rescue Palermo from the trivialities of the weekend broke next day, and was eventually to draw an excited crowd to the Piazza Ballaro, the area devoted to the food trade under the awe-inspiring silhouette of the ancient and gigantic church of Il Gesù. Manganelli had found a case that he could get his teeth into – that of a Mafia feud of the old-fashioned kind nowadays normally confined to unimportant provincial towns. This time it was in the heart of the capital itself.

A function of such piazzas is to provide a central, traffic-free area where business and pleasure, wonderfully combined, can be discussed in a leisurely and civilized fashion. Here in the Ballaro one of life's satisfactions was to waste as much time as possible outside a café, sipping a tiny cup of the wonderful coffee made by some illegal Tunisian immigrant. Normally by ten in the morning a vacant chair in the Piazza was as hard to find as a parking space in the Via Filangeri, but on this particular Tuesday, 24 March 1998, most of the cafés' habitués were crowded outside the premises of one Marcello Fava, the island's leading wholesale butcher. Press photographers pushed their way to the front, followed by a television crew and a number of German tourists shepherded by a guide, and soon it was no longer possible for latecomers such as ourselves to see what was going on.

Next day pictures appeared in the papers. The shutters had been pulled down over the Fava shop-fronts, and wreaths had been stacked against them on the pavement. Notices on the shutters announced Marcello Fava's forthcoming funeral, adding that floral tributes would be welcome. At some point someone in the crowd with inside information had broken the news to those standing nearby that the announced funeral was no more than a macabre, theatrical gesture, for Marcello was still alive, but would now be regarded as dead by the members of his family. What had happened was that ten days previously he had been arrested and charged with being the 'regent' of the Porta Nuova Mafia family and henchman of Vito Vitale, widely regarded as a future head of the Honoured Society despite being on the run for his numerous crimes. Facing the likelihood of life imprisonment Marcello promptly followed the example of Tommaso Buscetta, a leading *mafioso* who, finding himself in such a situation years before, had established the historical precedent of collaborating with justice in return for his freedom and police protection.

On the day when Fava's decision was made known his wife and four brothers went into mourning; the mock funeral was arranged and the business was to remain closed until this had taken place. It was pointed out in the press that 'transversal' vendettas were now the fashion and vengeance was executed on the families and relatives of *pentiti*, as they were called, who placed themselves beyond reach of punishment from their 'clan' by accepting the protection of the police. Hence the spectacular repudiation, the mock funeral, the wreaths – even the sermon by Padre Scordato, the local priest who while skilfully avoiding reference to the empty coffin made a somewhat opaque reference to Marcello Fava 'passing to a new life'. Nevertheless could it be, the family seemed to have feared, that their fiction of grief had failed to impress? This may have been the case, for shortly it became known that, whether they liked it or not, Marcello's wife and children had been spirited away by the police and placed out of danger 'far from Palermo'.

Manganelli's prompt and energetic response in this case was undoubtedly due to the belief that the *cupola* – the mysterious ruling body or council accepted as being in control of Mafia policy – had ordered an all-out attack on the growing number of deserters who had sold out to the police.

The Fava affair had followed close on the heels of a monstrous vendetta, the bones of which had been picked over even in the international press. This had exploded in the tiny crime-ridden town of San Giuseppe Iato, some thirty miles from the capital in the most poverty-stricken part of the island. The wretchedness of life in this place was complicated by the presence of two powerful and competitive Mafia families, both headed by psychopathic killers. One of these, Baldassare Di Maggio, had finally been arrested on a murder charge, and although unable to read or write, his presence made a deep and disturbing impression in the court. He was described by the prosecution as 'mysterious' and referred to as a schemer who not only killed his enemies but enjoyed dabbling in politics. When several years previously the former Italian premier and head of the Christian Democratic party, Giulio Andreotti, had been charged with involvement in the murder of a left-wing journalist, Di Maggio had gleefully described a meeting between the premier and the then accepted head of the Mafia, Totò Riina, reporting that the pair had exchanged kisses in Mafia style. This was dangerous stuff indeed, but Di Maggio had gone on to make things worse for himself by telling the press that he had been offered huge sums of money to retract but had declined to do so.

Faced with a life sentence in a prison in which overcrowding compelled four tiers of prisoners to tie themselves nightly into their bunks and where inmates sometimes quietly departed this life shortly after a gulp of the prison's famous 'morning coffee', Di Maggio followed Buscetta's lead and decided to collaborate.

The reaction of his local opponents, the Brusca clan, was to be foreseen. Di Maggio was held in a police stronghold where he blurted out the secrets of the Honoured Society plus those of a former premier who, although fallen from grace and currently on trial, still had powerful friends. Two months after Di Maggio's switch of loyalties his uncle and a cousin fell into an ambush. With that, all twenty members of his extended family publicly denounced him as a liar and refused police protection. Di Maggio's brother Emanuele, on his way back to town in the evening with his flock, was killed by fifteen pistol shots through the head. According to the coroner's report he ran two metres with at least one bullet in his brain before collapsing.

What seemed of most interest to the press in this case was the use by the assassin of a 7.65mm pistol of a kind unknown in Sicily, where such executions are conventionally carried out with the *lupara* – a sawn-off shotgun loaded with buckshot. As excitement spread, the general opinion was that this was the work of an agent from overseas. La Forte, the Public Attorney, commenting on the incident, said, 'It is to be presumed that all of you have heard of Cosa Nostra's military arm. Rest assured that we have precise ideas on the subject of those responsible for this crime, even if I am not prepared to discuss the subject in the press.' A profound silence on the subject was to follow.

In 1993 a low-level *mafioso* ally, Santino Di Matteo, became yet another *pentito* and turned against the Brusca clan. Following this his twelve-year-old son, Giuseppe, was kidnapped, held in an underground bunker near the village of San Giuseppe Iato for over two years and then strangled. The corpse was dissolved in acid. It was reported that in accordance with an ancient custom observed in such cases the boy's executioner bowed to the body before its immersion in the vat.

7

IN THE YEARS between my last visit to Sicily and this one in 1998, the excellent newspaper *L'Ora* had closed down. It had not survived the loss of its editor Mauro Di Mauro who had simply vanished one day, never to be seen again. Gioacchino was now a psychology professor at the University of Palermo, where he was regarded as an authority on the phenomenon of the Mafia. Among his publications recommended to me was a paper in English translation entitled *The Mafia Feeling*. I read this and learned a good deal from it, but reading it in the original decided that 'feeling' might not have been quite the word. *Sentire* was probably adequate in Italian, but I could not believe that its English equivalent could contain all those undertones of mystery, compulsion, intuition, obsession, frustration, hope and despair simmering under the surface of the original. 'The Mafia feeling' was neutral, devoid of rage. When Vito Vitale, Marcello Fava's boss, heard of the strangulation of Di Matteo's son, he was said to have shown little but anger that he, in his position, had not been invited to carry out the execution.

Gioacchino took Lesley and me to see Professor Franco Di Maria, head of department of the Faculty of Social Psychology at the University of Palermo. Both men were students of the Mafia, but extremely modest about the possible effect of their findings upon public opinion. 'Our hope,' said Di Maria, 'is that at least we can help people to understand.' The future, it seemed, was far from bright, and *Procuratore* Giancarlo Caselli had recently announced that he was afraid the situation was worsening. 'At most,' Caselli said, 'we are fighting a holding action. No more than that, and I absolutely forbid people to tell me that this criminal conspiracy with which we are faced is approaching extinction. Cosa Nostra has never ceased to be what it is now: strong, rich and organized – as brutal a beast as ever in fact, and it is at our peril that we relinquish the fight against it.'

Gioacchino's life on a left-wing newspaper had been ebullient and precarious when we first met, but now his struggle was to be continued on an ideological level together with his fellow professors at the university. The attack on the Mafia enemy was organized on a scientific level and in collaboration they had produced several major books on socio-political themes in which the undiminished Mafia problem was frequently ventilated. A recent paper of their authorship probes into a special mentality prevalent among the Sicilian people largely to be ascribed to the harsh vicissitudes of their past, plus a continuing infatuation with unsatisfactory role models from the West.

A Sicilian, agree the authors, may take a perverse pride in his Mafia allegiance because it dramatizes the circumstances of an unrewarding life. 'Here in Sicily,' Di Maria has written, 'the Mafia does not grow by forcing but in the most natural way, like a prickly pear which only responds to cutting back by an increased vigour of growth. To oppose it ineffectually only encourages its strength. Obedience to the group has always been considered a stronger motivation than any personal advantage, or the acquisition otherwise of prestige, and it is a sinister fact that a form of suppressed sympathy should exist among certain apparently respectable citizens. This results in penalties imposed by the law for Mafia-style offences being frequently less severe than those inflicted for common criminality.' For both men the traditional family remains the enemy to the evolution of a modern society, since it is so deeply engrained with the social patterns of the far past. A recent star in the dark firmament of the Mafia was asked the frank question as to why he had become a *mafioso* and replied in a way that was not difficult to understand: 'Because before that I was nothing, then I looked at my life and took it into my own hands. After that things changed. I went my own way, and now I have become a powerful member of a powerful group.'

Professor Di Maria told me of an ex-student who was a member of a powerful Sicilian Mafia family who wished to free himself from its control and discovered that this could only be achieved while living on the island by changing himself into a homosexual. By doing this he was able to escape the Mafia's deeply rooted influence. Most of his life was devoted to professional interests on the Italian mainland, and to recover his normal sexuality all he had to do was to go there. Whereas on the mainland he lived the life of a heterosexual, on returning home to Sicily he assumed an abnormal, but protective, homosexual role in an environment that demands above all *omertà* (manliness) of a male.

There were other aspects of the Mafia syndrome, Di Maria reminded me. Their history has been dominated by an inbred fear and distrust of all those in authority, and above all of the labour recruiters, the agents and officers of the feudal estates, the policemen, the gaolers, the lawgivers and their laws protecting the rich. The current heroes of the Sicilian bourgeois population are Falcone and Borsellino – brave judges who were destroyed by the Mafia, but in the minds of slum-dwellers or ruined peasants still cronies and protectors of the rich. These were no heroes to the adolescents from the slums.

Our talk turned to Calabria, the poorest of all the regions of mainland Italy. The Mafia code had now spread there too, carried mysteriously as if by proselytizers of a sinister new religion.

The Mafia had always been seen as a wholly Sicilian phenomenon, imitated elsewhere by minor and unsophisticated criminal associations lacking its organization, history and power. In residential areas of Naples, for example, each street had its saint lovingly housed in a shrine, on watch over the welfare but also the morality of its inhabitants, and thereby supporting a relatively trouble-free existence. The saints were often credited with exceptional powers, and when pushed could produce 'a miracle', as when marvelling crowds watched St Gennaro stop the lava flow from Vesuvius entering the city, merely by spreading his arms. Threatened with the wrath of a thousand or so of these protectors of Neapolitan virtue, the Camorra, the Neapolitan Mafia, was hardly more potent and significant as a criminal organization than a black-market operator who specialized in stealing the wheels off parked cars.

Further to the south and thus deeper into poverty and isolation, Calabria had its own second-rate criminal organization specializing in kidnappings and a watered-down form of Mafia terror. It had also become notorious for child miscreants – in Italian *I Baby Killer* – who had learned what they knew of the authentic Sicilian Mafia through a few much-censored and sentimentalized films. They were the victims of the increasing impact of a poverty hardly conceivable elsewhere in Europe – a new version of poverty based on intense unemployment in which the males of a family might spend most of their lives without work.

A school-leaver with no prospects of any kind might once in a while be given a few coins to clean out a barn, but the hunger of the young is not only for food, but for action other than time spent hanging around the local amusement arcade-cum-bar. For many juveniles their first taste of 'real life' in this Calabrian outback is gang membership even while at school. A matter of days before my discussion with Gioacchino and Di Maria news had come through of a gun-battle between schoolboys in the Calabrian town of Cinquefronda in which one boy had been shot dead. His twelve-year-old brother, a witness to the murder, could not be induced by any means to disclose to the police the identity of the killer.

At the root of the problem, both Gioacchino and Di Maria believed, were the values of the traditional Sicilian or Calabrian family. 'I give you my support,' the old-fashioned father is supposed to have intoned, 'and in return you will give me your loyalty.' And this, expressed in various ways, was the Mafia's view of the situation. In the past there was no human being to be discovered anywhere on earth less protected than the peasants who formed a vast proportion of the population of feudal Sicily. In this downtrodden mass, existing only to be exploited, the resolute, silent and implacable leader of a wholly acquiescent family tribe could at least better the prospects, however miserable, for all. If two or three such peasant resisters could sometimes secretly join forces, then so much the better. Thus secrecy, cultivated as a fine art, was key to a measure of success that could even come close to freedom.

An investigator into the origins of the word *mafia* was of the opinion that it dates back to the Norman conquest of the island and is derived from *ma fia* – the 'place of refuge' of Arab peasants of the times when they were rounded up for slavery on the invaders' new estates. If this is so, how strange and sad it is that from peasant resistance of the early Middle Ages Sicily should have inherited a title now applied to such masters of the art of exploitation and self-enrichment as Vito Vitale and Totò Riina.

If the power of the Sicilian family was the root of the trouble, for my professor friends the sensible remedy was to mount an assault against it that would weaken its grip on the nation. Their remedy was to increase youthful activity in every possible way. It was noted that with the exception of the worst case-histories in Calabria, most young people agreed that their schooldays had been the happiest times of their lives. Therefore, every effort should be made to extend school-leaving age, and to encourage sporting activities along with academic studies. Every plan that had as its goal the lessening of the family's bonds was worthy of consideration but in particular Gioacchino and Di Maria proposed an original and revolutionary project called the Solarium.

The Solarium proposed to send young people of both sexes on training courses in skilled labour. What was revolutionary in this case was that unmarried mothers were to be included in the scheme and taught men's skills. The University of Palermo had acquired two or three acres of abandoned land on the city's western out-skirts where a number of unmarried mothers, doomed in the normal course of things to an unsatisfactory and penurious existence, were to live with their children, in a state of independence almost equal to that of males. This was to be achieved by promoting cheap accommodation for them in socially pleasant and com-panionable surroundings, but above all by training them to acquire masculine skills. Thus they would enter a market previously wholly under masculine control, and might even expect to receive masculine rates of pay.

At first glance the Solarium was an encouraging name for a scarred industrial building consisting of little more than four walls set in what had once been a rich man's exotic garden. Originally a place of rare and even spec-tacular plants, it had now surrendered to the strangling of weeds. The basin of a fountain was rimmed by moss, and crow-like birds perched in the branches of rare trees and filled the air with their melancholic squawkings.

In these faintly depressing surroundings, however, the girl trainees and those who had completed their courses came as a surprise. They were already – or were to become – carpenters, joiners, painters, technicians and the rest, and appeared to be tackling whatever job they worked on with energy and high spirits. Instead of smocks and overalls, some of these girls were dressed as if they had looked in on their way to a party. Hairstyles were often elaborate and one girl operating a whining electric saw was festooned in gold chains. But most important of all was the mood of high spirits. Complimenting Gioacchino on the good looks of his operatives, I was overheard, and a cheer went up.

The atmosphere was wonderfully relaxed. The trainees were paid for their work. They ate cheaply at a restaurant with a permanently roaring television. Gioacchino agreed that to some extent this enterprise was part of a broader campaign to provide Sicilian youngsters with a public existence. At that moment, as if in illustration of his theme, a girl who would have been about the same age as those at work here passed with an older woman, possibly her mother, down the path along the Solarium's boundary. I could not help noticing that she did not hold herself fully erect but was submissively round-shouldered, as if by custom, like a figure in a shrine.

Returning once again to the subject of life in the Solarium, I said, 'At least they all seem very cheerful. Are there any drawbacks?'

'Not really,' he said. 'Having a little money to spend these days may make them more acquisitive. They probably don't eat as much as they should. The craze now is to save up to buy a mobile phone. They'll go hungry for a week or two to have one of those.'

8

LIFE IN SICILY tends to present itself as one under pressure of extraordinary extremes. The Sicilian is the legatee of an ancient and splendid civilization from which he has inherited human standards of an impressive kind. On the other hand he is also under assault by a species of social disease, the Mafia, for which no cure is yet apparent.

The Sicilians are fond of animals, particularly dogs and cats, for which public fiestas are arranged; there are weekly columns in the newspapers which are devoted to their interests. The writers are concerned with helping to provide their pets the most enjoyable of lives. Animal feast days are increasingly celebrated in the vicinity of the larger towns, and animal cemeteries are cropping up all over the island with arrangements for interments of all degrees of quality with appropriate headstones, inscriptions and floral arrangements. Nowadays cats are frequently cremated, although burial is usually chosen for dogs. The first funeral for a horse has recently been conducted, and more are to take place.

As well as their pets, Sicilians are interested in the

wildlife of the island, much of which, owing to its climate and remoteness from human interference, is rich and strange. Sicily possesses eagles galore, which are greatly admired. Recently a rare species was winged by a sportsman in the north of the island, and, after being in care for several months, the eagle was taken by plane for release over the wild, trackless and entangled woodlands of Ficuzza.

Wildlife reserves are being created at a feverish speed both in Sicily and on the Italian mainland, where they are now seen as helpful in the drive for tourism upon which the future of many of the remoter areas may depend. Of those already under development none is likely to equal in interest Lo Zingaro – a coastal strip running north from Castellammare del Golfo to San Vito lo Capo – parts of which through sheer inaccessibility were visited, until the last few years, almost exclusively by smugglers. The climate, rock formations and soil composition of this area of western Sicily produce a range of vegetation that is locally unique. There are flowers that grow only on this particular site, and a number of extremely rare birds. Here tall, spare, spindly trees with tiny, scintillating leaves thrust their roots deep among the rocks and the brine-soaked soil at the water's edge and dangle clusters of wan little blossoms among the strands of mist. It is a place of the softest colours. Human presence is recorded by ruined hutments of great age, and there are vast caves decorated occasionally with vaguely suggestive archaic forms.

We had arrived during the dry months in which Lo Zingaro is effectively sacrificed to pyromaniacs and this season, alas, had already produced several major fires. On 29 July 1998 an outbreak of fire raging in the central area of the reserve risked its reduction to ashes. But had this been a normal outbreak, of which a few are to be expected at that time of year, or was it a response to a rumoured refusal to contribute funds to the powerful local Mafia clan of Castellammare del Golfo? At the height of the conflagration a former director of the reserve had been charged in court with having received a bribe of 30 million lire for suppressing a contract for the services of two motor boats to collaborate with the fire brigade. From all the evidence offered it seemed likely that there were occasions when it suited the director's purposes for fire to continue unrestrained. Thus more of the rare trees of the Zingaro would have been burned to ashes.

Wildlife always came high in my personal interests and its exceptional endowments in this field always drew me to Lo Zingaro whenever the journey could be arranged. This was often a difficult business, as until recently, in bad weather, the area remained isolated at the end of third-class roads. Partinico, once also rich in rare fauna and flora, was relatively accessible, being only fifteen miles from the capital. Although less spectacular in what it had to offer, it was the next best thing – rich in such wonderful birds as hoopoes and bee-eaters, and in my early days in this region, of easy access to a sea rich in fish. Once there had been a flourishing Roman colony here, of which many traces remained, but in our times it was largely inhabited by poverty-stricken peasants, a prey to a Mafia of the cruellest kind keep-ing them in subjection through control of the water supplies.

Gioacchino drove us over to the town through a land-scape typical of western Sicily. It gave the impression that it had been fought over many times in the past for it was devoid of isolated buildings, and the few small villages, such as the bandit Giuliano's birthplace at Montelepre, had been built on the top of steep hills, or clung precariously to their sides.

'When were you last in these parts?' Gioacchino asked, and I told him that apart from flying visits largely to photograph birds, it had been twenty-five years earlier. 'A London newspaper wanted a piece about Danilo Dolci, and he arranged to look after me himself for about ten days.

'Partinico was the most awful place I'd ever seen,' I continued. 'Someone had been murdered on the night of my arrival and they'd left the body lying all night in the street outside the door of Dolci's headquarters, in which guests including myself usually stayed.'

'You have a surprise coming,' Gioacchino said. 'Some big spenders are living in the area these days. It's very much in the news.'

We climbed up into Partinico and for a moment I thought we had missed our way and taken a wrong direction. These were the suburban streets of any sat-ellite town of Palermo: rows of small, newish houses, polished handles on front doors and a pot of flowers here and there on a window-sill. I had hoped to be able to find Dolci's house, but Gioacchino had never seen it and we found ourselves trapped in a one-way system with no-parking signs until eventually we arrived at what was clearly the main street. At the entrance to this I thought for a moment I might have spotted the converted warehouse in which Dolci had worked – it was the only old building in sight – but a line of cars was following and there was no way of turning back to investigate. We pulled in at the second of two small squares, called (in English) the Fountain Adonis, above which church bells crashed incessantly. The walls of the square's only building were faced with polished marble and the counter of the café it contained was piled with cakes and brightly-coloured snacks. A private house overlooked the square and Gioacchino pointed at the railings of its balcony which even in these times were draped with cloth so as to protect the modesty of girls gathering there in the cool of the evening, and the males passing beneath from impure thoughts.

In and around the Piazza del Duomo shops sold sports clothes, fishing gear, ceramics and pictures of cottages with thatched roofs to an affluent class who had come there in BMWs and Alfas. Gioacchino mentioned that as soon as people settled down in such a town they invented little habits based on custom and leisure, and here it was the habit to park the car and stroll from one piazza to the other and back a number of times.

Meanwhile I continued my obsession with the sombre building from the past that seemed to have survived in the surrounding glamour until the brink of the Millennium, convinced now that it was the one in which Danilo Dolci's pilgrims from all over the world had been lodged.

I mentioned my conviction to Lesley and told her about the corpse left all night in the street outside, encircled by the police, as was their custom, by a chalked frontier line no one was allowed to cross.

'Would Dolci have been scared?' she asked.

'I'm sure he wasn't. In Partinico in those days you

saw a corpse in the street once a week. It upset him
that foreigners who had come to visit him from civilized
countries should be exposed to such experiences. A
body couldn't be officially moved until dawn. Sometimes if they could spare a man the police put a guard
on it to keep the dogs away.'

'How was he? I mean Dolci,' she wanted to know.

'In appearance he was tall and strong. A man who
smiled continuously. We used to go for walks together.
He was always on the lookout for a good hill to climb.
Not only was he a friend of the poor but he treated them
politely. He used to address beggars as Sir.'

'How did you come to know him in the first place?'

'I met him in 1963 through James McNeish who spent
a great deal of time with him and eventually wrote an
excellent book about his experiences called *Fire Under
the Ashes*. By the time I first saw him he'd had a lot of
probably unwelcome publicity through Aldous Huxley
calling him the Gandhi of Sicily.'

'What was his background?'

'He was a middle-class boy from Milan studying
architecture at the university and teaching literature at
the night school to students who were largely factory
workers. James said he was influenced by religious
revivalists at that time, in particular by a Don Zeno
who preached total poverty. Dolci, James said, had
experienced a personal revulsion against what he called
the shallows of intellectualism and set out to devote his
life to helping the poor.'

'So why did he choose Partinico?'

'I suppose because it was the toughest place he could
find, and there were more poor people here than elsewhere. In his book James says that at the time of

Danilo's arrival 2,500 out of 5,100 children in the area did not go to school. He watched with compassion, James mentions, while a man to whom he had given his coat immediately sold it and drank the proceeds. Someone told him of a Partinico slum called the *Spine Sante* – meaning the Sacred Thorns – which was supposedly the worst in Sicily. He immediately moved in and married an abandoned widow with five children.'

'Did you ever go there?'

'Sadly no. I was not invited to. Danilo may have thought I was too squeamish to tackle the experience. James mentions the mounds of dung and rubbish lying around like booby traps. Two of his neighbours got hold of a can of industrial spirit and drank themselves to death.'

'Who killed this man outside Dolci's headquarters?' Lesley wanted to know.

'The Mafia always does the killings.'

'Why in this case?'

'Probably because he would have been mixed up in the business over the Iato dam. They would have seen him as a troublemaker – one of those who had organized themselves to pressure the authorities into doing something about the water shortage. People like Dolci had difficulties with the landowners, who knew perfectly well that if something was done to irrigate the wasteland they'd lose half their workforce. You can be sure that Danilo got himself involved, and that would be the reason for dumping the corpse outside *his* door.'

'Looking at this place as it is now, it's hard to believe things like that could ever have happened,' Lesley said.

'Naturally, but it's impossible to imagine this town as it was. As soon as the sun went down it was absolutely silent. There were no street lamps, so it was quite dark. People went indoors and stayed there. The few that faced the gloom outside walked up and down in twos and threes with sawn-off shotguns held under the long cloaks they always wore at night. It was their way of showing how tough they were. The café stayed open at night to scrape a living from the odd customer. It had wall-slots instead of windows. The fellow at the door was an ex-lifer whose nose had been chopped off.'

'Why didn't the Mafia kill Dolci while they were about it?' she asked.

'There was no point in doing so. He was no danger to them and he was a likeable man who would express his point of view calmly enough and leave whoever he was talking to to think it over. It was the police the Mafia really hated, and thinking about it, that corpse dumped at his door might have been a police spy.'

We went on discussing Dolci and the Mafia, and I mentioned he had once said that it was the religious community who were his real enemies and spoke with such disapproval and animosity of his work. Shortly after he settled in Partinico he was picked up by the police and charged with being a political agitator. The basis of his so-called agitation and the legal action it provoked was his determination actually to employ Article IV of the Italian Constitution to serve the purposes of the poor. The article states: 'The Republic recognizes the right of all its citizens to work, and ensures the conditions necessary to make this right effective.' The device Dolci chose was a campaign of civil obedience – not of disobedience of the kind usually favoured by protesters. A local road had become unusable after heavy rains, and it had been made clear that due to a lack of funds it would not be repaired. Dolci's plan was to persuade the peasants to undertake the work on their own account. Sixty unemployed roadworkers began to drain off the water, clear the verges, and remove the rocks and earth left by landslides. With that a force of 250 police arrived, led by an inspector who was promoted to superintendent next day for compelling the unemployed to leave the road as it was.

'They put him in the Ucciardone! – in a cell containing forty-four other prisoners. When visited by his lawyer he told him that his only complaint was the number of bugs which prevented the prisoners from sleeping. Hearing of this, an aristocratic female admirer sent him a bottle of DDT which Dolci promptly returned to her "as there would not be enough to go round". His would-be benefactress then sent four more gallons for which Dolci returned his heartiest thanks, and those of his fellow inmates. Thereafter he made no more criticisms of conditions in gaol.'

Shortly after Dolci's release we took the last of our walks together, this time in an exploration of the great, glistening plain of Partinico. It was an area imbued with the mystique of pre-history that by a miracle seemed to have remained aloof from modern times. Here the civilization of antiquity drove back the desert and filled the landscape with a brilliant filigree of gardens. There is no place in the world that reeks more strongly of the remote past than this. Any house that is more than a hovel is the ghost of a Roman villa, displaying the wasted grandeur of a massive portico, cracked arch and vaulted interior. All around, the orange orchards of the newcomers spread their magnificent gloom, through which the peasants moved almost with stealth. Water, now the prey of the Mafia, gurgled everywhere through a complex of ancient conduits, splashing and cascading from the jaws of stone pythons into rimmed cisterns and ditches. Through Partinico's scent of dust and oranges struck coldly a rank odour of marshes.

The sea appeared here as a surprise a mile or so beyond this enchanted spot. It came theatrically into view from the top of a sand dune with gulls screaming all around, and it was different from any sea I had seen before: dove-grey in a flat calm but patched with the most refulgent blue. Thousands of the tiniest of black crabs scattered over the wide beach. It was a windless day and we watched as a shallow wave unrolled like silk all along the shore, reaching to within thirty yards of where we stood, then withdrawing with a faint rustle of sand. A short distance away the waves broke against high ground and from this we saw sea eagles manoeuvring over water so brilliantly blue in this spot that it appeared almost that lamps had been lit below the surface. The grey, flickering shapes of a shoal of fish were passing through and an eagle came fluttering down in the attack like some gigantic black butterfly.

Danilo was in his element in such wild places. It was here, he said, that he came to rest when he could – although rest in his case meant vigorous activity and, here on the Partinico foreshore, a boyish chase after the weird crustaceans of the beach that scuttled at twice our running-speed for their holes as we came in sight.

In 1998, Partinico was back in the news again with a drive for tourism. Its Mafia past, underlined by the reforming efforts of Danilo Dolci and the years he spent there, was beginning to fade. Its main street was bustling with cafés, bars, beauty salons, a gymnasium and even a riding school. One or two unsightly shacks on the town's outskirts had been pulled down. There seemed to be some hope that Partinico, with its legendary and even sinister history, would soon rival Corleone as an attraction for foreign tourists.

Corleone, of course, had the huge advantage of being featured in Francis Ford Coppola's *Godfather* films, but Partinico, apart from its pleasant surroundings, was much more accessible. Corleone was an hour's drive away from Palermo, Partinico an easy twenty minutes, but there was nowhere in the neighbourhood of either town to stay.

Determined to become part of the modern world, Partinico is changing rapidly. Every day, it seems, there is a new attraction: a pub-discothèque one week, a café bar with computer games the next. The order has gone out that the locals should smarten themselves up, although the complaint is not that they live too much in the past, but in the unacceptable present. From now on no one will be allowed to enter the *municipio* wearing Bermuda shorts, sandals or any garment incompatible with Partinico's standard of civic dignity.

An excellent and up-to-date guidebook to Sicily speaks of the town as coming from the same desperate mould as Montelepre, Giuliano's birthplace. Quite suddenly, within the last year, the description is out of date; instead it has become jestingly referred to as the Medellín of Sicily. For several years small amounts of *Cannabis indica* have been grown in the vicinity and in July 1998 a large area of surrounding territory was subjected to what Sicilian police now call (in English) a 'blitz'. Some four thousand cannabis plants were discovered growing in soil exceptionally suitable for their cultivation. The plants, between four and six feet in height, were skilfully obscured from sight by grape-vines and lemon trees trained to provide fences.

This was the eleventh such raid that year, yet it was evident that total success still eluded the police, for in September there were more raids, this time on young people hawking bagfuls of freshly picked cannabis by the roadside at the entrance to Partinico. Notoriety alone probably contributed to the affluence of the place. Few visitors are likely to have gone there in search of high-quality narcotics, and curiosity is more likely to have been the attraction in the case of a small Sicilian town absurdly described in a newspaper as a miniature version of the drug capital of Colombia.

9

AFTER A BRIEF excursion to the beach near Partinico where Danilo Dolci had taken me years before, we decided to avoid the limited road coverage of western Sicily at this point and return to the capital. But before leaving for Palermo we went back into Partinico itself for a snack and a rest. The drive uphill along the narrow street leading to the town's centre was even more congested than usual, with traffic jams behind carabinieri assault troops parked in vehicles at each end and groups of Pubblica Sicurezza police in the main street itself. The facts of the matter were explained by Pascuale, the English-speaking waiter at Trattoria Fontana. 'Vito Vitale showed up. His wife runs a farm down in the valley and he was seen down there last night. There's half a million lire on his head. He has a girlfriend living on the other side of the hill.'

'Think they'll catch him?'

'No. It happens all the time. How far you got to go today?'

'Just Palermo.'

'You're going to be stopped a few times.'

'What's so remarkable about this man? What's he wanted for?'

'Kidnapping and murder. You used to hear about Totò Riina all the time. Now it's Vitale. They say he's taken over. He used to come in here when he was a kid. I never saw him because at that time I was in the States. I wouldn't recognize him anyway. They say he's grown a beard.'

In between serving customers Pascuale was ready with more details of the career of their famous local criminal and I was struck by the familiar folklore of the case. It was exactly like that of other top criminals who have become legends. All have started life as poor boys. Vito spent ten years as a shepherd before venturing into petty crime. Like Calò Vizzini and Totò Riina he was illiterate, and what has in some ways added to his legend is the story that being chased by the police for the first time he tunnelled into a ton of horse manure, in which he remained concealed for three days until the hunt had been abandoned. Up until then – as so often is the case in aspirant *mafiosi* – he is described as being exceptionally devout, and the local priest, as frequently happens in Sicilian village communities, supported his application to be trained for the Church. The application failed for a reason which once again provides a momentary glimpse of customs inherited from the depths of the past – because he was believed to possess second sight. Later, on the threshold of manhood, he was charged with a series of violent crimes, and in 1995, having managed to escape while under arrest for murder, he was officially classed as *latitante* – a fugitive from justice – and he became one of the most wanted men on the island. As is the case with too many *mafiosi* in Sicily, Vitale's fugitive status proved no hindrance to carrying out his business as normal.

The reason for this state of affairs is largely because Sicily's two separate police forces prefer to go their own way rather than work together. This was a problem for those charged with the maintenance of order in Italy during the war. The carabinieri, organized in military style, had no contact with the Pubblica Sicurezza, the civilian police, and both forces refused to engage in any undertaking in which their rivals were involved. The system was retained up until April 1998, when Vitale had been at large for three years. He was seen as exceptionally violent and dangerous, and the two police forces finally buried the hatchet and planned a unified offensive. In this combined effort much larger bodies of men could be employed than ever before. The police also benefited from the aid provided by several *pentiti* who had agreed to collaborate. Their escape from prison had been arranged and they had been sent to keep watch in the Partinico district to which, this being his home country, it was believed that Vitale would sooner or later return.

The breakthrough came within days of our conversation with Pascuale. The news broke that Vitale had been having an affair with a glamorous cousin, Girolama Barretta (married, two children, husband in prison), and that she had recently been spotted in the vicinity of Partinico. With that, a force of undercover policemen, including two professional beggars, was put together, dressed in various disguises and given the task of spying on Girolama's every movement. It was soon reported back that she had made two recent appearances in Partinico where she had had her hair done and spoken to an estate agent about the possibility of renting one of the new houses going up at nearby Borgetto.

The news encouraged the police to carry their plans a stage further. Among the sophisticated innovations made available to the combined forces was a *cannocchiale*, sent over from the United States and described as the world's most powerful telescope, previously employed only in the Gulf War. The telescope's lens provided an enormous degree of magnification, yet the instrument could be easily concealed. From what the estate agent had let slip it was decided that the first trial of the *cannocchiale* would be at Borgetto. On delivery, however, it proved larger than expected, and several trees had to be dug up and replanted on the tiny mountain behind the town in order to screen the telescope with their branches. From among them the huge eye peered down into every window with blinds drawn back and upon movements of all kinds, even those of the larger animals.

Its field of vision included plots of unfinished buildings put up by a developer and a monastery at the roadside where a hill curved up into the town centre. After some days of unrewarding scrutiny a Mercedes with Vitale at the wheel pulled up at the monastery door. Girolama emerged and jumped into the car. The *cannocchiale*'s eye swivelled to follow them past a mile or so of unfinished building-sites to a house without windows and with only a single floor, in which Vitale had established his headquarters. When the police arrived to arrest him he showed a degree of calm bordering upon indifference and the photographs published next day show a faintly derisory smile on his lips. Vitale had little taste for luxury, and had lived as he preferred to in the austere surroundings of his Partinico family house. It was the Mercedes that was his undoing.

For some reason the Vitale case appeared to stir the Sicilian imagination, feeding in the normal way contentedly on a staple diet of minor drama, swindles and political chicanery. Visiting my favourite bar in Palermo that week for my evening drink, the talk seemed to be of little else. For a week or two pictures taken of the boss shortly after his arrest continued to be printed in the newspapers. He is seen wrapped up in what seems to be a duvet, from which only his face appears, wearing his somewhat Mongolian smile. His lips are drawn back to reveal a row of abnormally small teeth. Later there were more pictures of him, flanked by a supporting cast of recently captured bosses, several of whom have the same slightly Mongolian features, accentuated in Vitale's case by a moustache drooping from the corners of the mouth to the chin.

Asked shortly after his capture why he had chosen to conceal himself in a partially built house without windows or even a back door, he had replied nonchalantly that he preferred space to comfort. The headlines exultantly reported that he was now in a cell big enough for five.

It is generally accepted in Sicily that Tommaso Buscetta's collaboration with the law in 1984 marked the beginning of a new era in the war against the Mafia. Although the triumph of good over evil continued to be deferred, it had filled the island with *pentiti* collaborators, and also trebled the prison population. Spies and informers were everywhere and it was their enthusiasm and pertinacity, encouraged perhaps by small rewards, that led to the arrest and imprisonment of Vitale's fifteen-year-old son, Giovanni.

Two weeks after Vitale's capture the police arrived at the family home to carry 'the little boss', as he was called, off to prison. Two former members of the Vitale clan, now turned informers, reported that the superboss had boasted of his son's ability to take over command, and claimed that his boy had already accompanied him on an occasion when killings were carried out. Following this report a listening device was fitted in a car known to be used by Giovanni and young friends of the family. According to the police they recorded a conversation discussing a proposed extortion and an attack on a local inspector of the Pubblica Sicurezza. There were unexpected complications in trying to bring a case against the young Vitale, not the least of which was that he was a minor.

It was a case without precedent, and full of procedural pitfalls. How could a minor be legally accepted as a *capo-mafia*? The decision was finally reached that in order for the hearing of a charge of Mafia-association to go ahead the doors of the courtroom would be 'thrown wide' in accordance with the ancient law of Norman origin: *Porte Aperte*. The tribunal was called upon to provide 'visibility' of its procedures and findings to all members of the public, who were thus permitted to assist at the trial. These were present while Giovanni Vitale was charged with *oltraggio* (outrage), violence and wounding. Added to this he was accused of 'leaping' to assume command of the Partinico Mafia and of passing on orders given to him by his father when he visited him in gaol. Giovanni Vitale was then committed to prison while awaiting trial.

Questioned after his arrest, the boy had denied all charges, insisting that on the date stated on the charge he had spent the whole day helping with the family's cows. He was nevertheless taken to the Malaspina prison and placed in solitary confinement. His mother, Maria Lo Baida, had been refused permission to visit him. Appealing to an assembled crowd, she said, 'My son is a serious boy who studies geometry in his second year and is at peace with his conscience. We're humble people who live in a humble house.' His grandmother, also present, said, 'I seem to be in a madhouse. This child has been put away just as if he were a criminal, when he's no more than a baby who wouldn't harm a kitten.'

The chaplain of the Malaspina prison, Father Enrico Schirro, announced that he wished to see the boy and remind him that Jesus loved him. According to the press, the chaplain added that prison was the place where the individual confronts his conscience and that the silence of the cell can promote the most profound meditation and thus the restoration of the soul's balance.

It was perhaps inevitable that, notwithstanding the success of their first combined operation, something would happen to damage the new and happy relationship between the two branches of the police. No sooner had the wonderful telescope been dismantled and re-packed for return to the United States than it was rumoured that once again the separate divisions were at daggers drawn. It was now said that the much-publicized tracking down of Vitale through his amorous cousin – and thus even the use of the telescope itself – had been a meaningless propaganda exercise. In fact Vitale's capture had already been arranged through an informer of the Pubblica Sicurezza. To which the answer should perhaps have been, what did it matter how, and by whom, this man was captured so long as, after so many years, he had at last been removed from circulation?

Dear Customer, please take a moment to provide contact information.

1. Contact Name _____

                              (a person not traveling with you today)

2. Contact Phone Number _____

                                (include country code, area code and number)

3. Are you a U.S. Citizen   Yes ☐   No ☐

4. I decline to provide this information. ☐

This information is only retained for 24 hours and will remain confidential. Thank You.

(W) L0/90

NORTHWEST
AIRLINES

WORLDWIDE KLM NORTHWEST RELIABILITY

FIRST CLASS SEAT   WORLD BUSINESS CLASS SEAT   ECONOMY CLASS SEAT   DEPARTURE GATE

Boarding Pass

FLIGHT/DATE   DESTINATION   CONNECTION   POINT OF ISSUE

NW0167 V 01MAY03   SEATTLE/TAC   MSP/BWI/0187

PASSENGER'S NAME

HAWKINS/WILLIAMENE

All Customers; Please provide contact information on the reverse of this boarding pass.

640012
3COPS5

ETKT ETKT ETKT

ETKT ETKT

STAPLE HERE

INSERT

06/01 (M) PRINTED IN CANADA BY MERCURY GRAPHICS •••• REV. 09/98

IO

MANY PLACES OF special interest to me were in the less accessible west of the island, which through poor communications was little influenced by the outside world. An immediate problem arose. It is an area more or less dominated by Corleone – the only large town – and its sole hotel, recently opened, had only stayed in business a few months before being closed down. There were several small towns in reach of Palermo to be visited – one of these, San Giuseppe Iato, was currently filling the newspapers with accounts of its bloody feuds – but we were put off making short trips from the capital by the traffic jams that imprisoned cars entering or leaving Palermo both in the morning and evening.

A solution was proposed by Marcello's sister-in-law, Gabriella, in a suggestion put rather cautiously as if she was not quite sure that it should be made. Renowned in Palermo as the leading artist in the creation of theatre backgrounds and effects, Gabriella lived alternatively in the heart of the city and in a forest retreat on the margin of the famous and somewhat sinister Ficuzza wood, some twenty-five miles from the capital. This was the only woodland to survive in Sicily since the island's deforestation by the Romans and such was its reputation that when on a previous trip I had mentioned to Marcello my intention of visiting it he had emphasized the necessity of my employing an armed guard.

Gabriella was by nature adventurous. Ficuzza, she said, defeated the tameness of normal existence. She knew of a place nearby where we could find a room. 'It's rather private. All the people who go there know each other. They don't take to outsiders. But if you feel like staying there I'll do my best to arrange it. Just keep on going until the road stops, and you'll see it where the trees begin. It's very small and quiet. We call it the kingdom of silence.'

'Sounds just what we're looking for,' I said, and we set out.

The guidebook still speaks of the road running south from Palermo to Agrigento branching away 'into bandit country' and passing through 'some of the finest inland scenery that Sicily has to offer'. This is an understatement – certainly in the opening days of spring. There were no houses, villages, people, animals, trees, and little by way of scenery but vague mountain shapes scribbled on milky skies. Further on, vast, immaculate, although almost colourless valleys offered surrealistic tableaux of rocky outcrops, tiny pyramidical mountains capped with enormous crags and, once, the image of a castle in miniature, appearing then dissolving in wraiths of mist. This was the earth as it had been in the depths of the past, before human interference. It was also the former heartland of the Mafia, as described by the guidebook.

Our approach to Ficuzza was through Godrano, a village wound round a hilltop with its oldest houses perched on the edge of a precipice with a tremendous view of a tree-choked ravine far below. Here the houses are of the kind known as *bassi*, consisting of a single room with a wide door opened as required to let in the light, although resourceful occupants will have knocked holes in the walls themselves to serve as glassless windows. This village is too poor to possess a shop. A van, we were told, arrives once a day and was there at that moment, alerting the inhabitants to its presence by a few bars of oriental-sounding recorded music – indistinguishable so far as I was concerned from the Muslim call to prayer. In the cold spring weather the road verge sprouted innumerable tiny blue flowers and in the gorge below owls hooted, like the sound of crying children, in broad daylight. A story put about locally was that the villagers were the descendants of an ancient non-European tribe, that many suffered from colour-blindness, and that sickly children were fed by them with thimblefuls of blood.

Il Rifugio, our destination, came into sight at the end of a downhill mile full of twists and turns – a grey little fortress of a place at the very edge of the forest and within sight of Ficuzza itself. Men were at work in a nearby shed chopping logs. With their unnaturally large muscles and empty faces there was something about them that spoke of forebears whose lives had been used up down the centuries in this way. Four large, unkempt dogs made a stealthy approach, heads fastidiously turned away. They were of a strange, square-jawed breed with yellowish eyes – of a race as old perhaps as the forest itself. Behind this scene the rays of the early evening sun lit up a façade of tall oaks. A deep lane had been cut through these and in the far distance the forest closed in on a gloom approaching that of night.

I showed the man who ran the inn Gabriella's note and his expression changed as though a key had been turned in his brain. 'You are from the Signorina,' he said, opening the door wide. The room we were shown into was awash with the scent of wood smouldering in a vast hearth. At this moment the landlord's wife was busy in her cavernous kitchen preparing the evening meal which, as was the custom in these parts, the man of the house would eventually cook. Both were slow, bulky, watchful and uncommunicative, and there was an emptiness about the building emphasized by the distant slamming of heavy doors. We saw only one other guest, an elderly lady of slightly ethereal presence who appeared at frequent intervals to make small changes in the position of the room's moveable objects before withdrawing from sight.

Everything in the atmosphere and mood of this place differed from our experience of Palermo and the north. These quiet, unemphatic, reserved people seemed of a different race – and perhaps they were. Antonio, the owner, listened attentively to whatever was said to him, and replied with the minimum of words. He was constantly in physical action, sawing up branches to feed the enormous fire or preparing a meal for which the ingredients were cut up with a kind of surgical skill. Later, more unsmiling guests arrived and were seated at separate tables where they engaged each other in low-voiced conversation. At intervals of fifteen minutes these mutterings were submerged in the chiming of a clock, almost as powerful as that of a church.

After an early supper we went out to look at the view, which except for a single corner of the horizon was largely of trees, but five miles to the south the Rocca Busambra thrust its enormous tombstone bulk up through the woodlands. This ashen breach in the deep greens was dyed by the sunset almost to the colour of blood. It was here, I remembered, that the remains of Placido Rizzotto, an anti-Mafia trade union leader from Corleone, had been brought to be thrown down a hundred-foot-deep crevice. Visiting it two years later, the fire brigade brought up in their first sack five shoes, a pair of braces, an ankle bone, a piece of overcoat and a human head. The head had been lying in the mud and the features had gone, but Placido's father recognized his son's chestnut hair, and also a piece of his overcoat. He had only had it made the year before, 'with buttons down the middle in the new fashion'. Further searches by the fire brigade produced more sacks full of bones. For many years this had been the hiding place of bodies of the men of Corleone who had fallen foul of the Mafia.

'You'll find it very quiet,' Gabriella had said of Ficuzza. She was right, but the vicinity of Il Rifugio generated sounds of its own: the muffled yelps with which the dogs signalled their presence as they patrolled under the walls through the night, the mewing of the owls, the thump of the inn's heavy doors, and above all, through the windows, the dry lisp of the wind from all sides of the surrounding thickets. The inn itself had inherited a perpetual hubbub from the Middle Ages – of pots being washed in the enormous sink and the woodsman dragging in heavy branches to hack to pieces on the stone floor.

Gabriella had come to be accepted by these people after a long fascination with the tribal intricacies of Ficuzza. She told us that the surname of all local families was Lupo (Wolf) and that the Wolves were divided into two clans, the White Wolves and the Black Wolves. Of these, the Whites formed the upper crust, voted for the party of the Church, listened to taped opera music and ate white bread. The Blacks supported the Popular Front, hummed or whistled tunes one might have heard in the mountains of Morocco, and forced themselves in hard times to chew on the flesh of the prickly pear, which although nutritious was revolting to the taste buds. Woodsmen who spent their lives hacking up oak trees were Black Wolves, but the owner of the village café who sat in an armchair waiting for the telephone to ring was definitely White. A scientist from Palermo claimed to have found a difference in the thickness of the cranial bones of these two clans but the locals were supremely sceptical about such theories and poured scorn upon his views.

Ficuzza's days of fame and fortune had depended upon its having been chosen in 1800 by King Ferdinand to be the site of his palatial hunting lodge, still perfectly preserved in its gardens a couple of hundred yards back from the village. The King, well known to be infatuated with boar-hunting, had been told that for devotees of the sport no area could compare with this one. He came here whenever he could and, supported by a regiment of soldiers, killed a hundred or so animals a day. His arrival was a mixed blessing for the local people, who had always hunted here for their own food. This was now classed as poaching, and punished by the amputation of both hands, most poachers dying immediately from shock, or soon after from loss of blood. Some cattle had also been brought by the royal household to Ficuzza, and there were cases of hungry peasants cutting collops of meat from the cows, then sewing the skin back to cover the wound. For this the punishment was branding, and by Sicilian law of the time the poorer the offender the severer was the punishment to be inflicted. Some probably garbled accounts of these happenings had survived in local folklore but I was distracted from further historical investigation by my desire to see Corleone again. We cut short our visit, packed up and set out.

I I

APART FROM THAT brief visit with Gioacchino in
1990, it had been years since I had seen anything of
Corleone and now I found it tremendously altered. New
suburbs had overflowed at the top of the hill and huge
sales stickers half covering the windows of shopping
parades had reduced the slightly sinister surroundings
of old to an environment which was no more than
ordinary. Supermarkets full of bargains had opened as
well as health-food shops selling an enormous variety of
witches' brews made from the organs of such animals as
salamanders and snakes.

In spite of its unsavoury history, the town had gained
a new respectability. Our friend Gabriella had spent
time there and praised it for its clean streets, quiet nights,
mountain views and fresh food. These calm virtues
were not enough, however, for Corleone's citizens who
were intent on refurbishing the town's image by adding
fashion and drama, and publicity experts had been called
in to advise how this could best be done.

Their solution was imaginative: the Sicilian Regional

Government invited a Danish couple, Christina Hansen and Kenneth Jorgens, to celebrate their wedding at Corleone and, accompanied by twenty Danish journalists, they duly arrived to be pelted with flowers by schoolchildren dressed in typical local costume. Following the ceremony the newly-weds were offered lunch in the Piazza Garibaldi – tagliatelle con ricotta with grilled sausages, described in the press as a typical Danish meal. The Danish consul then spoke, dismissing accounts of past Mafia atrocities as 'a pernicious legend from which Corleone has so long suffered', and he was loudly applauded. This, it was clear, was a festival of mealy mouths; nevertheless it was judged a huge success. The happy couple planted an olive tree and departed.

Christina and Kenneth, we learned, were to be followed by an adventurous Japanese pair, who it was hoped might be induced to complete the last lap of their journey by balloon. Negotiations were afoot, it was said, to entertain them with the first showing in Italy of the film *Titanic*.

In the matter of press coverage this had been a good day for Corleone, but the one that followed was less satisfactory with the town again back in the headlines. A seventy-four-year-old man called Francesco Gambino, describing himself as a healer and magician and said to have a large following of believers, had been driven from his home; his two cars (one a BMW) had been set on fire. In the course of the inquiry it was stated that Gambino, 'noted for his long pigtail and his extravagances, has twenty-five children by four wives, the youngest child being a baby of two by a girl of twenty-one'. He kept his house full of chickens and other domestic animals used in his cures. The attack was prompted by neighbours who could no longer stand the smell. He was charged with 'abuse of credulity and ignoring hygienic laws', and is considered to have exposed himself to the risk of extra-legal action on grounds of immorality, this being in the eyes of the Honoured Society one of the cardinal sins.

Since my last visit the Ministry of the Interior in Rome had sent a commission with special powers to take over Corleone. It had succeeded in suppressing muggings, burglaries and petty thefts, and the municipality's present claim is that it is one of the few large towns in Europe where cars parked at night may be left unlocked. Thus encouraged, solid Sicilian bourgeois moved in, in no way dismayed by the open and continuing presence of the Mafia leader Totò Riina, who walked its streets unmolested despite twenty-three life sentences, none of which had been served.

I saw Riina only once, when a journalist arranged for me to glimpse him through a peep-hole in a cell wall of the maximum-security prison of Termini Imerese. Riina had deigned to occupy his cell for an hour or two and, clad in a silk dressing gown, was dictating a letter to his beautiful secretary. When news broke that the State had been paying Mafia bosses pensions while in prison or on the run, the name of Totò Riina inevitably appeared on the list. He claimed to be *nullatenente* – a sufferer from extreme poverty – but the newspapers reported that among his possessions were land, apartments, villas and jewellery.

Someone had tried to persuade me when last in the town that the famous *mafiosi* one might occasionally run into were now in retirement. 'They're just here because they like the place. Corleone is the Oxford of

Sicily. These are sentimental attachments no one wants to break.'

Sicilians have always believed that banks help to ease backward towns like this into the modern world, and three had been recently opened. Almost everyone I spoke to recommended that I visit the museum, another symbol of modernity which had recently opened. As an experience this proved to be less stimulating than we had hoped for. The door was locked and the lady curator arriving with the key discovered it would not fit, so the lock had to be forced before it would open. Even then the effort proved hardly worthwhile: the only exhibits of interest behind the dusty glass were the fossilized penis of a prehistoric man and a stuffed cockerel of striking deformity.

The old town, reached with some difficulty through traffic congested narrow streets, remained largely unchanged and as depressing as before. It was still topped by a singular natural phenomenon in its centre in the form of a towering outcrop of rock. Locally this has been explained as a result of the collapse a few million years ago of part of the earth's crust, leaving only this monstrous column unaffected. At the time of my previous visit the effect had been all the more eerie due to the fact that the town gaol had been built on its summit. Nowadays it is perhaps less disturbing since this building is occupied by an exceptionally unworldly order of mendicant friars. One of the Brothers is famous for traipsing barefoot from end to end of the town comforting citizens who have suffered from the continuing presence of evil.

In an effort perhaps to improve the town's image a 'commemorative act' was staged in memory of Placido

Rizzotto, the first of Sicily's trade union leaders, who had been abducted from this spot exactly fifty years before. He appears from all accounts to have been among the most attractive Sicilians of recent history, and the public commemoration occupied three days with the Piazza Garibaldi constantly full to overbrimming. All the usual public figures were there, politicians appeared from all over the country, famous actors delivered funeral odes, a hundred or so island communities had sent representatives, and the survivors of one of those old-fashioned sisterhoods who could weep to order had been tracked down to contribute their own speciality. This they did in the most moving way, on and off, for the whole three days.

After half a century of near oblivion Placido was at last to be recognized for the hero he was. When hardly more than a boy he had distinguished himself fighting with the partisans in northern Italy before returning home and throwing himself into the struggle to assist the browbeaten peasantry of Corleone.

In 1947, elections were to be held for the first time since the coming of fascism, the only issue of importance being the peasants' demand to occupy uncultivated land. But for the Sicilian poor there was even less hope in 1947 than there had been in 1943. Mussolini had been on the verge of destroying the Mafia, but then he had fallen, and all the *mafiosi* had been released from prison. The victorious Allies replaced all the existing mayors with *mafiosi* and the Sicilian peasants' cause was lost. The order went out from the Mafia that everyone should vote for the Christian Democrats, and, as it was generally believed in Corleone that there was no such thing as the secrecy of the ballot, it was to be assumed that most people would. But, to be certain, numerous safeguards were adopted by the party of the landowners and the Mafia. Dr Navarra of Corleone, for example, issued several hundred certificates of blindness or extreme myopia to local women who were then escorted by *mafiosi* to the polling booths to make sure they voted Christian Democrat. Despite these precautions, and to general surprise, Corleone elected a left-wing council, largely thanks to Placido's efforts.

Out for a stroll in his favourite haunt on 10 March 1948, Placido Rizzotto was kidnapped by two men carrying pistols and marched away into the hilly country outside the town. He was never seen alive again, except by a frightened shepherd boy who left his herd and came running to report that he had seen two men hang a third from a tree.

12

I WAS EAGER to revisit Mazara del Vallo – on the south-west coast of Sicily and one of the most charming of all Mediterranean towns – best reached on this occasion by by-roads through a landscape that seems largely to have avoided the twentieth century. This is yet another area much affected by a drop in rural population following the human haemorrhage of the immediate post-war period, when the United States opened its gates to the exploited peasantry of southern Europe. Tens of thousands of peasants took the opportunity to escape the age-old tyranny of the Sicilian countryside. A half-century of slow leakage of people from one continent to another had left emptiness and silence in many villages along these meandering roads. Even the dogs of old had gone, and sometimes only two or three houses gave signs of occupation. Farm-carts slumped on broken wheels in a courtyard strewn with ancient debris. Barn doors fell away from broken hinges and sometimes even the remnants of decayed harnesses hung from walls, although the horses were no more. The village shops had closed down, deserted by the last of their customers, and a traveller in these parts could be in difficulties because there were no road signs and no one was available to point out the way.

Most of those who refused to emigrate made for already overcrowded towns where they shared the poverty of the original inhabitants, half of whom lived below the poverty level. Remarkably Mazara was exempt from such melancholy statistics. Its citizens had never been toilers on the land, for the Carthaginians who built the original city had chosen the site for its proximity to the richest of Mediterranean fishing waters, and it is a source of wealth that has never declined. On all counts Mazara is to be admired for its elegance and its calm. It is a ghost of a corner of the French Riviera of old, with a promenade and palms, grotesque old cars with squeaky horns kept by their owners out of affection, a background of baroque churches of splendid proportions, and even a Norman cathedral to which a baroque façade had been added. This town is notable in Sicily for its civic pride and, apart from helpful directions displayed for the benefit of visiting strangers, the municipality has done its best to foster good manners and a caring attitude among its citizens by the discreet posting of notices saying no more than *Cleanliness and Civility*. They had obviously been effective, for Mazara turned out to be indeed a civilized place where nostalgia was blended with imagination and even a touch of showmanship. The lengths to which its people were prepared to go to be kind to strangers was exemplified by the response of a driver caught up with us in a traffic jam, whom we asked for directions to our hotel. 'You'll never find it,' he said, and turning his car around led the way through the traffic to look for it at the other end of town.

We arrived shortly before dark in time to enjoy a pleasant local phenomenon frequently experienced in such conscientious Sicilian towns. Clumps of trees with suitable foliage are planted along quiet streets and above all the sea-front parade, if – as in this case – one exists. At sunset, in the absence of other roosting sites in this treeless country, these attract innumerable small birds. We stood outside the hotel and watched thousands arrive, settling to screech happily and twitch their wings among the leaves. It was a performance repeated in all the trees planted along the promenade, producing such a localized din that within a few yards of a tree it could be heard above the noise of the traffic.

Our arrival in Mazara coincided with news of a sensational find in local waters. A bronze statue had been hauled off the sea bottom in a fisherman's net and had immediately become the subject of intense discussion between experts sent to Mazara from various Italian cities, including Rome.

The statue, said the man at the hotel desk, was roughly two metres long, and had been seen by a friend shortly after its recovery from the water. It had first been accepted as a representation of Aeolus, god of the wind, but this opinion had been rapidly discarded and it was now generally known as 'The Dancing Satyr'. It was supposed to have been on the seabed since about 400 BC, and was much damaged. The story was that this unique archaeological treasure had been caught up in the nets many times before and simply thrown back. My friend found it ironic that what had been no more than a nuisance to local fishermen was suddenly regarded as of such importance that it had to be locked away out of sight and could only be inspected by permission of the municipal authorities – this being granted only in the case of accredited experts. Many people, he said, were of the opinion that this was the result of a conspiracy originating in Rome. It had been stated locally, he went on to say, that the processes of restoration would take a minimum of two years to complete, the first stage being a six-month immersion in fresh water in an attempt to reduce the action of the salt that had penetrated the metal. He passed me a blurred newspaper photograph showing the statue immediately after recovery. It looked no more than a shapeless object covered in seaweed and slime.

By this stage other members of the hotel staff had gathered to listen to our conversation. They did their best to show enthusiasm for this remarkable find, but could not disguise the fact that what really mattered to them was where the statue would be restored. Mazara possessed a properly equipped laboratory, used on many previous occasions for restorations of this kind, so why should the city be robbed of its statue? There were hints that Palermo might lay claim to it, but it was even more likely that Rome, with its political clout, would brush all local opposition aside and move in to take over.

The local view, including that of the hotel staff, was that after restoration the statue should be allowed a permanent home in the cathedral. But now, quite suddenly, this had been opposed by influential members of the community. The assistant manager, who was passing through, stopped to join the discussion and explain why this should be so. After a general clean-up, he said, the statue's detached leg had been temporarily replaced in position. This, it was found, emphasized a posture already described as 'orgiastic', thus – as he himself believed – making its presence inappropriate in a temple of the Christian faith.

The grace and splendour of Mazara failed quite to conceal the presence of a strange phenomenon of the kind least to be expected in the sprucest of cities. The grandest of its buildings, the castle, cathedral and several of its most imposing churches, are clustered at the south end of the promenade, and behind it in the Piazza della Repubblica, described by a guidebook, much given to overpraise, as 'perhaps the most beautiful in Italy'.

An after-dinner stroll there was to produce the surprise of a lifetime. The visitor is surrounded by superb ecclesiastical buildings, normally immaculate in their pale limestone but on this occasion defaced with graffiti up to the height the tallest vandal could reach. These were no mere scrawlings but legible inscriptions carried out in white or red paint. It is possible that technically speaking they could not properly be described as graffiti – the appellation normally applies to the primitive and incoherent drawings disfiguring walls in many parts of the world. These were plain, unadorned statements, usually of distress, and evidently in most cases the work of adolescent girls who wrote of the transports and miseries of sex – sometimes in a single blasphemous sentence, but also almost at essay length. Now came the real surprise, for in almost every case English was the language employed. 'Shield me from the sight of this man again,' one wrote. 'My life is in ruins.' 'How long will God allow me to be left alone?' another appealed. 'Let us turn our backs on each other and walk away,' wrote a third. But why, we asked, should English be chosen by these superbly educated young sufferers as the language of hatred or love? We would never know, but of one thing I was certain: whatever was written here across so many square yards of wall was well constructed, well spelt, pithy and concise. There was no doubt about it, Sicilian language teachers were of the best.

Here in Mazara people led a good, bustling life, a result, I suspected, of a long process of human trial and error sifted out slowly over the centuries from what had been on offer by the ancient world. This was a great place for human contact. The young were to be seen everywhere locked together in amorous oblivion at bus stops. Everyone carried a mobile telephone. The locals were generous; when I tipped a waiter he dropped a picture of the Spice Girls by my plate. At sundown all the old men came out and stood packed together, two deep along the main street's eighteen-inch-wide pavement, to enjoy the sight of the traffic going by. Mazara had taken 2,500 years to become what it was.

Mazara was an old town, but Gibellina, thirty miles away inland, was the newest in Sicily. Gibellina had been knocked down along with every other village in a couple of hundred square miles across the Belice River by the 1968 earthquake – the last of many in an area of chronic seismic disruption in which the ancients had been clever enough not to settle. The old Gibellina had been left as a pile of rubble, and construction of a new town started several miles away. This, it was announced, was to be 'unlike anything on earth'.

The description was impossible to resist, and we drove through rolling, treeless country to reach the new Gibellina in an hour or so.

It came almost as a surprise, isolated among sparse olive groves and patches of abandoned land. The streets into which we shortly drove were wide and quiet and we saw only a few pedestrians before we reached the centre of town. What had become of the estimated population of five thousand? There was an overall impression of space still to be filled and in the architecture of what had been so far completed the feeling was of an ardent search for novelty of shape and colour. We passed a fountain shaped – by intention, as we were later to learn – like a lock. Houses were outstandingly angular. Some, perhaps the first to be built, were painted in strident colours, which later lost out to black and pastel shades of all kinds. But this introduction to the city of the future was short-lived; we were soon in an area where the brave-new-world effects had surrendered to an urban standardization, which appeared in this context surprisingly out of place.

The approach road swung in a wide curve down into the centre and here the town planners had set out in earnest to *épater les bourgeois* with what appeared as a small park enclosed by a low wall painted with vast imitation graffiti. These, I suspected, had been based on photographs taken in some lively slum. It was an idea that had failed, because whereas the originals would have been created with the determination of provoking distaste, or even rage, these, offered solely as decoration, could stimulate little but boredom.

The town came down to earth with a Spar supermarket much like any other, but there were no customers in sight, and the lady at the check-out appeared at first glance to be asleep. The only attempt to liven up this area of the city was a huge ragged shape cut out of tin supported on a pole, which after the first few days of being on view could not possibly have been accepted by the residents with more than indifference. It would have been interesting to have had facts and figures about Gibellina – how many houses were occupied, how long was it on average before a new houseowner decided that it was time to move on, and what the residents did for a living – and to have been able to study the proposals of those who had planned it. We tried the information office but it could not help. Its leaflets were about tours to Venice and Rome, but little else. Nevertheless the man in charge had one piece of cheering news. 'You can park here wherever you like. Nothing to pay.'

The verdict then, was that as a living, working, expanding town it was non-existent, because its purpose had gone. But this must also have been true in the case of the town's predecessor that was wiped out by the earthquake, which must also have been by then at the end of its natural life. A handful of the occupants of the new Gibellina could presumably commute by car to Mazara, but where else could they find work, for what was there to do here? The earthquake of 1968 that had laid the old town in ruins had in effect only accelerated what was already happening. By that time much of the population, having passed so many years in the drudgery and poverty of feudal agriculture, had already made their escape.

13

FROM A GLANCE at the map I could see that Villalba, capital of the rural Mafia in the old days, was not more than a two-hour drive across country at this point. Here, I thought, was a place that would have been caught up in – perhaps even obliterated by – the flood-tides of change, and in a burst of curiosity I decided the time had come for a second visit.

Villalba of old had been the undisputed capital of the unkempt and uncouth old ex-farmer, Calogero Vizzini (Don Calò), known to the Allies as 'General Mafia' due to his effective assistance to the American Seventh Army following their landing on the south-east coast of Sicily on 10 July 1943. A British contingent had landed too, but mistakenly had advanced against tough enemy resistance up the eastern coastal highway, involving them in a month's delay and the loss of several thousand men before reaching their objective at Messina.

In the west, the Americans, choosing a difficult and mountainous route, had taken only seven days to bring their part of the campaign to a conclusion. Their only losses had been through minor accidents of various kinds. The Axis defenders surrendered at Mount Cammarata, and Don Calò, having managed the campaign from behind the scenes, now arrived in a U.S. tank. He had only recently been released from Mussolini's prison to become mayor of Villalba, and now, travelling westwards with the advancing Americans, he busied himself by replacing existing mayors in the towns successively occupied in the advance by others of his own choosing. From then on the Mafia, at that time suffering a wasting sickness, began to recover health and strength, but in a new form: the old rural version of the Honoured Society was doomed and Cosa Nostra, imported with the American troops, was on its way.

In July 1943, when Don Calò had waved from his tank to the welcoming crowds, the Mafia had been a rural phenomenon sucking leech-like at the blood of the three-fifths of the population condemned to live on the land. Another decade was enough to spread the cancer cells of Cosa Nostra not only to the outskirts of Rome, but to establish a vigorous satellite in North America specializing in the manufacture and distribution of drugs. The headquarters, however, always remained in Palermo.

In the early days of this process of expansion and change, Villalba, birthplace of so many villainies, lost whatever purpose it had ever possessed, unable to adjust its life to the future or to fulfil any of the functions of the past. To see it again, physically unchanged after the passage of thirty years, came as a surprise. There it lay, spread out at the base of the rolling hills, an austere cross-hatching of white streets, low buildings, small windows, and high walls. Women wandered into sight, wrapped in black shawls. Old men walked on the bandy legs of the past. A scattering of teenage boys appeared to create annoyances in the emptinesses of crossroads, then disappeared. A single customer sat facing the street, as they always did in such cases, in the doorway of the only café in sight.

The town lifts itself slowly to its central square with a fine baroque church at one end. The church steps lead up to a platform from which Don Calò, always slovenly and dishevelled, would describe the benefits of hard work and raise his hand to be kissed. Facing the church at the other end of the square, a benchful of old men studied an inactive fountain. A priest walked by in the little black pyramid of his shade. A bell tolled and the intervening silence was broken only by the remote cackle of crows in the sky. Could this place be in the same country as the new Partinico?

The war had opened its arms like a saviour to Sicily, for after the landings there were few battles to be fought. The armies, heading for the north, drew the corruption after them, leaving Villalba purged of recent miseries and extortions. Even the cruelty of labour in the fields was at an end, although once again Villalba was re-nailed to the cross of tradition, and where only a few decades back vast horticultural prairies had occupied human energy from dawn to sundown, now only an occasional old man was to be seen turning over the earth in his cabbage patch with a spade.

My first visit to Villalba had been too late to experience the adventure of a meeting with Don Calò Vizzini. A Sicilian friend had, however, enjoyed the rare privilege of being presented to the Mafia chieftain on the famous day when Vizzini met U.S. Army officers in the main square. Describing his appearance on this occasion, he said that Don Calò was as unkempt as usual, in baggy trousers and a rumpled shirt, although a partial transformation had been attempted by persuading him to put on an officer's jacket with sleeves that were far too long. Vizzini, my friend thought, took some perverse pleasure in his slovenly image, a well-known form of Mafia affectation. Some months before this he had actually appeared in public with unbuttoned flies, causing a young girl who was present to titter. On being rebuked by his angry gesture she had lost the power of speech for a day.

The incident was seen as another evidence of this illiterate ex-farmer's almost hypnotic power over his fellow humans. Local worthies, including a baron, had been summoned to Villalba to welcome him and the Americans, but Vizzini had virtually ignored them, the baron being dismissed with a wave of his hand and the request to find someone to look after his dog.

Despite this arrogant showmanship there was no doubt about the keenness of Don Calò's brain, his insight into the manipulations of local politics and the spell he exercised over the poverty-stricken peasants who tilled his land. He was seen as useful by the local landowning aristocracy, who emulated the system by which he kept the lower classes in order. They frequently invited him to join in social occasions in their houses, but such invitations were never accepted.

As the American force began its advance to the north Vizzini's knowledge of what lay ahead, of the German defenders' positions and failing strength, and the weakness of the local authorities about to be replaced by *mafiosi*, was invaluable. The whole campaign was completed in a matter of weeks, although some two years were to pass before democratic rule would be restored in the Sicilian south.

Two years or so later Don Calò died of a heart attack after a prodigious celebratory meal following a political triumph of a friend. He lay in state in the local church and leading personalities of the government and the Church and heads of all the Mafia families came to pay their respects, and countrymen from local villages flocked to Villalba where they slept under hedgerows or in the street. It was characteristic of such an event that the newspapermen present, even those from the capital, referred in their coverage of the occasion to the almost overpowering fragrance of Don Calò's body in death. The funeral notice displayed on the church door said that, 'Wise, dynamic, tireless, he was the benefactor of the workers on the land and in the sulphur mines. Constantly doing good, his reputation was widespread both in Italy and abroad. Great in the face of persecution, greater still in adversity, he remained unfailingly cheerful, and now with the peace of Christ and the majesty of death, he receives from friends and foes alike the grandest of all tributes: He was a gentleman.'

Photographs in the press show Don Calò's successor, Giuseppe Genco Russo, who had been his second-in-command, standing beside Don Calò's body under the flowers heaped up on his bier. They are separate, but in other photographs Russo is seen to be connected to his former chief by a cord. It is down this cord, according to a Mafia article of faith, that the vital fluid from the corpse flows into the living body which from that moment on will inherit in its entirety the power and genius of the dead man. Russo's participation in the ritual strengthened the theory that the origins of the Mafia were pre-Christian rather than dating from the Norman conquest of Sicily.

14

THOSE WHO HAVE had the opportunity to see the Roman mosaics of Piazza Armerina may conclude, as I have done, that there is nothing of the kind to compare with them elsewhere on earth. Throughout the summer months the Villa del Casale is under siege by tourists from all over Europe, two thousand a day being deposited by buses in the main square of the town. After a brief exposure to local hucksters, they are snatched away by the waiting guides to be force-fed into a narrow gangway suspended from the villa's roof. From then on, shuffling forward a foot at a time, their peregrination ten feet above floor level takes them round 12,000 square feet of the mosaics' revelation of the life of the Roman aristocracy in the third century AD.

An immensely rich man – possibly the Emperor Maximianus himself – built the villa in this area, chosen in all probability by reason of the splendour and variety of the game it provided the hunter at a time when many of the animals shown in the mosaics had already become extinct on the Italian mainland.

In Sicily

On the walls of the villa are recorded the pleasures and excitements of the day. These Roman patricians banquet, hunt, fish, celebrate religious feasts, race in their chariots, kill their enemies and make love. Their children imitate them so far as they can – hunting small animals, and even driving in miniature chariots drawn, according to these pictures, by large birds. Bejewelled princesses consult their mirrors while officiating at religious ceremonies. Ten tall, slender ladies appear in bikinis. Once described as enjoying themselves at the nearest lido, they are now stated to have been athletes, one of whom is shown as about to be crowned for her performance.

What is extraordinary is the realism of these tableaux. At third-century Piazza Armerina we are close to the threshold of the ice age of the Byzantine ikon and its mass-production of roughly identical, dehumanized faces. These men, women and children of Piazza Armerina share our emotions and react as we would have done in the situations recorded on these walls. Encountering a wild boar – or even a lion – the hunter's concentrated wariness is drawn from the life. In the face of danger the struggle is also with fear. Children's eyes bulge with terror when attacked by fighting cocks. Suffering has never been more convincingly depicted than in the face of a giant struck by an arrow, or the alarm of a plebeian, his yoke of oxen out of control, under the stony gaze of his superiors. Ulysses, offering drink to the Cyclops Polyphemus, wears a servile smirk, and the anger of a child being whipped by a bully is fiercer than that of a grown man in battle. Only one erotic image was on show: the rear view of a woman in the arms of her love. Her ample buttocks protrude from voluminous garments. Her head is turned sideways and their lips meet in a kiss. Neither seems more than mildly surprised. Never in this portrayal of the ancient Romans in Sicily is a smile to be seen. Could it be that – as in patrician Sicily even now – laughter was considered ill-bred?

In May 1998 the Villa del Casale at Piazza Armerina was defaced by mysterious intruders who poured a quantity of black varnish over one of the pavement mosaics. This outrage, occurring a week before our visit, sent a shock wave of horror throughout the island, and was stated to be the second such act of sabotage to have taken place. There were two more to come. The damage had been done late at night when what sounds like a primitive security system had broken down, although a camera had managed to record the presence of two presumed culprits. Most Sicilians were perplexed as to the purpose of the operation, for nothing had been stolen, and even regarded as a piece of vandalism it appeared pointless, for it was unlikely that permanent damage had been caused. Poised on the gangway above a black splash covering most of the body of a running man, it seemed reasonable to suppose that special skills would be required for the varnish to be cleaned away – but no more than that.

But who had been responsible for the attack, and why had they gone to the trouble of breaking into the villa to do no more than this? Several viewpoints were put forward and defended with some emphasis. Inevitably for the benefit of the headlines the vandalism was attributed by the newspapers to the malevolence of Cosa Nostra, by which name the Mafia is inevitably known when spectacular misdoings are involved. Even General Conforti of the Palermo carabinieri said, 'I believe the Mafia has its paws in this.' But in what way, others asked, was the world's most powerful and effective criminal association likely to benefit from inflicting trivial damage on a work of art? However, Gian Filippo Villari, superintendent of the villa, seemed inclined towards the general's viewpoint. He reported threats made by mysterious telephone callers, and a dog with its throat cut left at his door. Mafia or not, Villari went on to say, this was a situation which could be improved upon by providing more money to deal with the staffing problem and to install an up-to-date security system.

The somewhat farcical attack on the mosaics drew public attention to a far more pressing problem in the Piazza Armerina area. This was the widespread and virtually unchecked activities of numerous tomb robbers. Excavations at the ancient Greek city of Morgantina, ten miles from Piazza, have uncovered a large agora, a theatre, a sanctuary of Demeter and many more mosaics, and such treasures as the Aphrodite of Morgantina, now in the Getty Museum in California. This site appears as an earlier and smaller version of Piazza Armerina itself, but owing to its relative isolation is virtually at the mercy of thieves. Narrow roads radiate from it in all directions into the woodlands and hills. The mayor of a small town in the vicinity spoke of the dealers who dig up antiques to order, and apologize for having to keep a customer waiting for a month or two for an acceptable statue, 'although we can probably do a nice necklace from stock'.

For our expedition to Piazza Armerina our original intention had been to hire a self-drive car in Palermo, explore the area described in these discouraging reports, put up for the night in a local hotel, and return next day. But since then Lesley had damaged her hand, obliging us to take a taxi instead. It was this complication, plus a report that a party driving after dark in the vicinity of Morgantina had actually seen persons digging by lamplight at the roadside, that made us decide to scrap our original plan and return by taxi to Palermo on the same day.

I was later to read the views of an art historian called Ignazio Nigrelli on the plunder of Morgantina. 'With every year that passes,' he wrote, 'the incomparable Sicilian heritage continues to waste away.' He recalled his disillusionment when the moment arrived to publish his collection of photographs assembled over the years under the title 'Works of art from Piazza Armerina, lost, dispersed or at risk'. Whatever had survived, he said, was to provide the nucleus of the town's future museum but in fact by the time his work on the volume was complete all the objects in it had disappeared. 'They vanished. This was the end of my hopes.' Nigrelli's anguished protest was seized upon by the Sicilian press, which also published the views of the American archaeologist Malcolm Bell, who affirmed, 'without a shadow of doubt', that a collection of fifteen pieces of 'priceless treasure' dating from the third century BC, now in the Metropolitan Museum of New York, had been illegally dug up between Morgantina and Enna. With Bell's help, the authorities hoped to bring these 'monuments of antiquity' back to a Sicilian museum.

According to Gian Filippo Villari such illegally obtained objects were normally smuggled into the United States via Switzerland, and up to fifty times the price paid to the grave-robbers would be received, no questions asked, on delivery to a foreign museum. General Conforti added masterpieces by Caravaggio and Rubens stolen from Sicilian churches to the list of missing works of art. He was sceptical whether any of them would be returned in the near future.

The relentless worldwide hunt for the buried treasure of antiquity was delayed to some extent in Italy until Mussolini's downfall, which not only freed the Mafia from pressure but contributed to the expansion of their operations. Morgantina, practically unheard of until 1960, was to be invaded by collectors when the news that squatters in an old house had found forty-four gold pieces dating from the fourth century BC under the floor. 'That's when all the digging started,' our driver had told us. 'It wasn't much of a place until then. No money about. They used to keep the goat in the kitchen at night.'

15

ONE OF THE radical changes we noticed in Palermo, compared to our previous visits, was the large number of African immigrants in the city. Indeed their numbers, and the authenticity of those claiming refugee status, had become a major talking point. Subject to investigation, genuine immigrants arriving in Sicily were allowed a period of thirty days while it was decided whether they should be allowed to stay on or returned to their country of origin. If the applicant's appeal was turned down he or she would be served with a *foglio di via*, providing a further fifteen days' grace for additional enquiries, before, if necessary, a final expulsion order was issued. This delay may have been intended to deal with endless muddles in a humanitarian fashion; for whatever may be one's opinion of law and order in Sicily, it is a country where remarkable generosity – even when unexpected or undeserved – is frequently encountered. It is not unusual to meet foreigners of a half-dozen different nationalities doing their best to turn themselves into Sicilian citizens, and on the whole such applicants are treated with sympathy. The problems are complex and the regulations change virtually from week to week. Nevertheless many of the hopefuls are in the end lucky in their endeavours.

Complex legal discussions were taking place once again all over Sicily as the 'immigrant season' approached. A bewildering number of forms had to be filed in the offices of the carabinieri and the Guardia di Finanza, which dealt with these unsolicited invasions. Was an applicant desiring to stay in Sicily the innocent victim of religious persecution, or a member of a generally banned political sect? Having put through a claim for residence by 22 Moroccan dissidents, how, in this homeland of muddle, is the chief of police expected to react to the news that the number of applicants should have been not 22, but 122?

Across the water in Tunisia the winter rain had been once again less than hoped for. The general view was that in the absence of a prolonged, last-minute downpour people were in for a hard summer, with the income of the poorest Tunisians dropping as low as one-eighth of that of their counterparts in Sicily. These were the worst times south of the Mediterranean in many memories, with the earth seeming almost to be drying out. Rain or no rain, Sicily, as possessor of some of the richest soil in Europe, always came off best. By early spring, along the African coast they were already doing their best to patch up the old vessels kept for such emergencies, ready to fill them with half-starved peasants and ferry them at night across to little sheltered bays on the south-eastern coast of Sicily where the sympathetic

Sicilians would put up with having to fill a few extra mouths for a while, and do their best to find the refugees some work to keep them going.

By the first week in summer it was clear that one of the familiar tragedies of the past was about to be repeated. Quite apart from seaborne invasions from Tunisia, increasing numbers of Algerians, Moroccans and even Pakistanis began to appear in Palermo, Agrigento, Syracuse and other coastal towns where they gave no trouble and were grateful to be employed in any occupation that could be found for them at substantially less than the going rate of pay.

The peak period for such illicit landings is early August when, after a few unpredictable storms, an almost glacial calm falls upon the water, and the small and vulnerable boats are launched from the African beaches. When they fall into Sicilian hands, such vessels are routinely described in the Maritime Police registers as 'in precarious condition', and this accurately describes the facts. They are also very old, one in 1998 being identified as having featured in a regatta at Palermo some forty-five years before. Complicated repairs are frequently carried out upon such vessels while still at sea. The worst possible nightmare that can befall immigrants – or occasionally tourists on such voyages – is that a fever will strike out of the blue, malaria being the most frequent. This is also the preoccupation of the Sicilian port authorities who await arrivals with a certain degree of pessimism.

When a flat summer calm is expected to hold up for two months, Lampedusa is the favourite destination. For the natives of this island it is a hard-working place, dry in summer, treeless and scourged by winds.

It has excellent beaches, expensive hotels open for a short summer season, and the reputation of being the kind of place to go to get away from it all. Middle-level politicians favour it and the fishing is said to be the best in the Mediterranean. When the tourist season ends naturalists descend upon the place to study an exceedingly rare turtle that can be attracted by a species of supersonic whistle, breeds only once in its lifetime and lays its many eggs in the immaculate sand.

The news of the African invasion was soon worse. A second boat had arrived carrying refugees, not only from Tunisia but from Egypt and – astonishingly – Sierra Leone. Two cases of malaria had been established already and a further 160 illegal immigrants were suspected of carrying the disease and had been under observation for two weeks. With that, the hotels closed down.

As always, the reports were full of wild inaccuracies. In Trapani the notorious expulsion orders intended to clear the town of disorderly immigrants were employed. Something went badly wrong, however, for although the immigration authorities claimed to have located two thousand clandestines, the order was only used in five cases. Murky operations in matters of food and trade were to be suspected behind the scenes. That powerful figure the Official Assessor of Agriculture for the Sicilian region furiously demanded to be told if honourable Sicilians had suggested a deal involving the exchange of penniless immigrant labourers for Sicilian olive oil. He rejected such a possibility with scorn, although it appeared that many did not. There was a view that some African authorities would have been happy to ship out as many of what were regarded as unemployables as they could. Islamic fundamentalists, too, were beginning to make a nuisance of themselves in some Muslim countries and might have been got rid of by their authorities as indentured labourers. A few rich Sicilian holidaymakers in Lampedusa caused offence among the local people by criticizing poverty-stricken refugees for being improperly dressed.

The last phase of the invasion broke all records with the arrival via Lampedusa of three hundred desperate clandestines. There were several more malaria cases and medical services at Lampedusa reported back to Agrigento: 'We have a single ambulance and two doctors only.' Alarm was signalled in other Mediterranean areas, and nine Egyptians suffering from an undiagnosed sickness were refused entry to Malta.

At Syracuse an avalanche of desperate refugees managed to get ashore. In the ensuing manhunt seven policemen were hospitalized, along with a similar number of refugees. Some of the detainees complained of feeling ill, convincingly describing symptoms of malaria, but on investigation this proved to be a better than average hoax. However, a number of refugees were genuinely ill and the leader of the Moroccan fugitives at Agrigento, having been taken to prison, died in his cell.

Now, with the waning of summer, the outlook down in the port was more hopeful. The surrounding waters came to life. Strong gusts of wind swept the birch-broom branches of the few trees and water gurgled and was swallowed in the deep basins in the rocks. The boats which had lain motionless until now began to bounce about on the waves in a lopsided way and the boatmen shouted advice in high-pitched voices to those who manoeuvred around and through those already tied up. The summer scent of sea-rotted wood was blown away by the breeze.

Soon Sicily was gripped by something close to panic. The papers reported that 250 cases of infection had been reported at Agrigento and large boats were bringing in yet more from Tunisia, Libya, Syria, Morocco and Iraq. In Lampedusa an ancient democratic procedure was utilized to settle the question of whether or not persons arriving from African ports should be permitted to land. It was put to the vote, and 40 per cent of the islanders agreed that they should stay. Of the remaining 60 per cent almost all had not bothered to register an opinion.

At this moment when Sicily was overrun by refugees from the impoverished South a newspaper thought fit to employ a well-known journalist to describe what it was like to be one of thousands of displaced black men who had come to the island in search of work and food. Giovanni – whom I had met briefly at a journalists' rendezvous on the harbour – had written a slim book on the colour problem which had made very little impact. He had, moreover, reached the conclusion that as a white man he was debarred from a real understanding of the troubles undergone by the immigrants. Now, in response to his editor's suggestion, he decided to turn himself (as far as this could be done) into a replica of a black man put ashore at night somewhere along the coast, with no more than a few possessions, and confronted immediately with life in a great city where it could be hard indeed to earn enough to survive.

It had to be admitted by all concerned that some initial cheating had come into this. Palermo's leading theatrical make-up artist was engaged to change the colour of Giovanni's skin. Released from this man's studio he was at first hardly recognizable even to himself. An hour or two earlier he would have been seen as no more than a reporter keeping a watch on the morning crowd in the Via Lincoln della Marina, and trying to think of something to write. Now along with his colour even the shape of his head seemed to have changed, and studying his reflection in a shop window, he was reminded, he said, of a poverty-stricken African onlooker at the camel festival at Ain Sefra about which he had once written a piece.

With his brown skin and cast-off clothes from the flea market he was committed to scraping a living in competition with destitute Africans at the very bottom of the human market. From preliminary enquiries he had learned that this involved polishing the windscreens of cars trapped in the innumerable traffic jams of Palermo, and then selling the driver a cheap lighter or a scratch-card purchased from wholesalers specializing in such junk. Even in the case of such simple occupations there were skills to be learned, and the competition was intense; nevertheless these were the only activities in the city in which the Mafia took no hand. Experts, most of them black, who had followed this trade for years, knew everything that was to be known about which were the best places to operate. The windscreen-polisher spots his prey stuck at the lights, dashes in, gets to work on the screen, then hopes to persuade the driver to buy a scratch-card or lighter in exchange for the work he has done. The method is to catch a car with a full sixteen seconds left to work on before the lights change to green and it hurtles away. Allowing himself a day to study all the variables, Giovanni had learned that an accomplished polisher managed to score in one case out of six. Above all it was essential to avoid annoying the driver by being too persistent over the loss of a potential sale.

There were many lessons to be learned, the first being that as a black he had become invisible. Previously, in the briefest of street encounters, there had always been an instant of mutual scrutiny. In his new avocation this had been lost. Almost in his first few minutes as a black pedlar he had lost his human identity, and his presence was no longer registered. Palermo, he learned, is not racist, but merely wholly indifferent to coloured people. Other friendly invisibles or semi-invisibles taught him where and with whom to try his luck with a car, and thus something about cars themselves, but far more about human nature. Sales were low there, but if you accepted that any reward was better than nothing you found out that the Piazza Giulio Cesare was the place. The drivers there drove old Fiats and were poor, but comparatively rich in humanity and usually good for a few lire. He was warned to avoid drivers in the smart Piazza Croce ensconced in the air-conditioning of their BMWs who corrected the focus of their eyes to infinity at the mere approach of a black man. You polished the screen, then sometimes without recompense there was an imperious touch of the horn and the rich man departed.

Thus the day passed. On the scorching afternoons he sweated profusely but could not wipe away the perspiration because of his make-up. Tired, he longed for a coffee after an endless morning's work. But despite everything he'd learned he still had not fully grasped what is acceptable in a black man, and what is not. Seating himself like any normal customer at one of the small tables provided by a bar, he noticed the waiter's stunned expression. It was one of those places to which, apart from customers, only sellers of roses are permitted access. He realized he was no longer invisible. Instead of coming to take his order the waiter went to talk to the owner who, seated at the other end of the bar, was heard to say, 'Ask him what he wants.' The English learned so many years ago at school came to Giovanni's rescue, as he replied in that language, 'Black coffee if you please.' Despite another startled expression from the waiter this was instantly served.

The afternoon was a poor one for the windscreen-polishers. It was one of the hottest days of the year with patrons in the open-air restaurants dropping off to sleep in their seats. Traffic was very light, with cars expertly parked in the small spaces everywhere, as if for the night. It was five in the afternoon before a few cars appeared. Giovanni sold three scratch-cards and, suddenly overtaken by hunger, found a place down in a cellar at the back of the San Domenico market where he exhausted the day's income on two pig's trotters.

After that, the problem was where to sleep. Despite the temptation to call on one of his colleagues to beg a bed for the night he chose to sleep in the shelter for down-and-outs in the semi-slum of the Albergheria run by the aged Silesian priest Don Meli. This time his highly professional make-up threatened to cause a problem. He had interviewed the priest, regarded locally as a saint, on several occasions and saw him as a friend, but due to the old man's deafness, his weak eyesight and the make-up, Don Meli failed to recognize him. 'We're pretty full at the moment,' the old priest said. 'It'll have to be just for the night, and you know the rules. Up for a wash-up at five-thirty.'

A single day was enough to provide Giovanni with the experiences he had to describe, and to teach him that those scratching the most meagre of livings should not polish windscreens of BMWs in the Piazza Croce but stick to Fiats driven by egg-dealers in a less glamorous square. Human kindness in its manifestations in Sicily is richer – probably as everywhere – as one descends the human scale, but even there the poor man is almost invisible to the rich. Nevertheless the generosity and good grace with which the island's working people take in so many foreigners in distress, whatever their colour, cannot be surpassed anywhere else on earth.

16

IN PARTS OF the south Mediterranean vestiges of an August fair remain, commemorating the Great Emperor as well as hailing the traditional triumph of midsummer. In remote Sicilian villages where a little of the past still shows through, the Sicilian Ferragosto, as the fair is called, still survives, and a few very old and perhaps confused people dress for its entertainments and ceremonies as if for church. The big towns can afford to do the thing in style with processions and firework displays, but the most destitute of the villages struggle to contribute their mite of thanksgiving and mirth as best they can. Danilo Dolci helped his neighbours to assist in meagre celebrations in the drab surroundings of Partinico, and even at Favara near Agrigento, where Mussolini was so shocked by Mafia excesses, celebratory horse play at Ferragosto was attempted. Where local prosperity reflects an excellent fishing season or even a record influx of tourists, all work for a day or two comes to an end and Ferragosto reigns supreme. Millions of cars seem to take to the roads, and average speeds in the neighbourhood of the big cities drop to three miles per hour. A huge, almost frenzied rush to the beaches takes place, where the bodies stretched out there are sometimes separated in the most popular areas by no more than five inches of sand. The population of the small scatter of the Aeolian Islands north of Sicily increases from 1,200 to an estimated 25,000, prices rise two and a half times, and up to six tourists are occasionally called upon to sleep in a single room.

The only island to have lost visitors in this season was the volcanic Stromboli, where we watched an eruption in the manner of the most spectacular firework display, although in 1998 the opening of a new crater, filling the night sky with its sparks, came too early to ruin the holiday proceedings. The year, apart from the new crater and its fiery outbursts, was remarkable for freak rainstorms. The temperature, rarely less than 100°F, fell in an hour by thirty degrees, but this was nothing compared to the situation in Palermo, where cars dragged themselves through liquid mud coursing down the gutters of its narrow streets.

Above all, given the right age, company and opportunity Ferragosto is accepted as the time of romantic adventure, when young men and women respond with awakened interest to impulses too often numbed or suppressed in the average working life.

While we were in Sicily the reputable and somewhat conservative *Giornale della Sicilia* published the extraordinary statistic that 67 per cent of Sicilian married couples are unfaithful to one another, adding the even more astonishing rider that in the case of *both* sexes these infidelities are often committed with prostitutes.

There are a number of areas, some already mentioned in this book, where sexual encounters take place in cars – frequently in broad daylight – in narrow one-way streets where there is little or no passing traffic, and it is probable that a proportion of these adulteries occur there. The newsmen noted that the peak period in one such street coincided with the midday break, and that the turnover was rapid. It was thought that in some cases the spirit of adventure came into the thing, for as one investigator reported, certain males, although by no means short of money, derived a perverse satisfaction at the idea of being paid for sex by a woman – however small the sum involved.

Apart from such well-known streets there is nowhere within reach of the romantically minded to compare with the Parco della Favorita – the small unspoilt wilderness holding back the houses where Palermo comes suddenly to a stop, and the ancient trees climb into the crags of Monte Pellegrino overhanging the city. It is a scene that has turned its back on the years, remaining part of a past that is fading rapidly. The separation between the two areas comes suddenly and is complete. Within yards the rumpus of traffic is smothered in the leafy cloak of the forest. With the arrival of summer one or two eagles return, and sometimes come floating into sight between the peaks. Prints made by Palermitan artists a century and a half ago show these surroundings just as they are now – a superb trysting place reached on foot within minutes from the road to Isola delle Femmine, and thereafter screened from the alien eye.

There appears at first to be no one in the forest,

although there are always people about, moving stealthily among the trees. These are often *luccioli* (fire flies), black prostitutes from one or other of the impoverished countries of North Africa. They are usually in search of work of any kind, but are driven through the lack of its availability to take up their present occupation. No census can be taken among this dense woodland but with every year the numbers increase, although this passes almost without notice, for the *luccioli* dress in green garments matching the forest glades, and they are unobtrusive and well behaved as they lurk silently among the spread of leaves.

There is a single striking fact about the *luccioli* that so far has received no wide publicity in Sicily although it is accepted in the Muslim countries from which many come. This is that they are regarded as bearers of good luck. It is a credence that has assumed spectacular form in some areas. In the mountains of Algeria, where I spent five months of the last war, men of intelligence among the local population frequented prostitutes not so much for physical satisfaction as in the belief that they were the possessors of psychic powers and could cause their enemies to disappear. In the mountains behind Philippeville (now Skikda), spring was celebrated by the arrival of a kind of super-prostitute inhabiting for a few days a shrine among the trees. She had a small retinue of attendants and was treated with enormous respect, a lottery being organized among the local tribesmen to determine who would be the first to have sex with a partner that in origin must have been a local pre-Muslim goddess of fertility. A long list of suitors followed the winner, upon whose successful conjunction, taking up to an hour to complete, depended the tribal fortunes for that year. Each of these presented *en nisa* – the holy prostitute – with a gold coin, with which he bought not only love, but *baraka*, good luck.

Prostitution by black *luccioli* has established itself in Sicily largely since the war. When I first went to the island at the end of hostilities its presence was discreet in the extreme. Then slowly over the succeeding years the coloured girls began to appear.

'Where do they all come from?' I asked a journalist friend.

'Ghana, Nigeria, Morocco, Tunisia. Even Sierra Leone, I believe. The poorest countries. This is like the kingdom of heaven after Mali, with its diet of brown rice, two or three handfuls per family a day.'

'Would you say you see many more about the place than you did a few years ago?'

'Oh, many more. Maybe two or three times as many. Most of them don't have papers, but they get away with it. The police just look the other way.'

'What's the attraction for the Sicilians? I suppose you're going to tell me they're cheap.'

'Well yes, I suppose, but it's not only that. The real thing on the whole is that most of them are nice people. It may be because they started out poor, but they're well brought up. Their mothers warn them, "Don't be greedy." They come over here and maybe work for two or three months before they get picked up by the police and sent back. They've usually put by a few lire to help with the family situation at home, and then when funds run out they come back again.'

'Don't the police do anything about it?'

'They've too much on their hands as it is without having to bother about a few pros. I've talked to girls who've been served with an expulsion order a half-dozen times. They always come back. They see it as a holiday when they go home. A family meal and fresh chicken and souvenirs all round, and they're on their way back here again. Why should the police care? Half the foreigners working in this country don't have documents anyway.'

'Speaking of Sicily, would you say there's any drawback in being black? Are any of their customers put off by their colour?'

'Not in my opinion. If anything I suspect it's the reverse. Some of them probably get a kick out of it. At first, anyway. A friend at the university told me about a professor who's only interested in the black ones. And look at the fuss about that film Roberta Torre is going to produce with a Nigerian girl in the leading part.'

'Joey, you mean,' I said, 'but surely it's off? Didn't I read that they've put her back in the Trapani camp?'

'Yes, but she'll be out next week. They've already put a billion lire into the project. They're not going to lose out on a certain winner because someone's taking a few weeks to fix the papers. Roberta Torre can't talk about anything else right now. Of course they'll fix the papers. Of course she'll do the film and it'll break all box-office records.'

'A film about a black prostitute,' I said. 'I still find it incredible.'

'The thing is there's nothing crude about it,' my friend said. 'This isn't about being on the game for the money. It's about sacrifice. She's doing it for a starving family. In the end she'll marry a Nigerian husband in a proper church ceremony, and he'll love and respect her all the more for following the call of duty.'

My friend showed me Roberta Torre's description of

her protégée in his paper. 'She is a young, black goddess, as graceful as a gazelle,' the producer had said, and was on the point of embarking on a brilliant future. She had been obliged to live in a way that no girl would chose, but had changed everything, even a name nobody could pronounce. Now, as she went out to face her new life, she was to be Joey.

An immense publicity campaign was under way, said my friend. The fact that Joey was temporarily in custody at Trapani was of slight importance. With regular employment guaranteed by the film company her release was certain in a matter of days.

By coincidence it was precisely at this moment that Syracuse was faced with a crisis in which *luccioli* were heavily involved. As a busy port its population of prostitutes was inevitably high. They were part of the accepted life of the town. Cheerful and well behaved, and often appearing, according to Roberta Torre, in the crowds down by the station as 'little oriental princesses.'

The station – also part of the port area – was the centre of the current problem, for it had always been accepted as the meeting place of the *luccioli* and their potential clients. Now suddenly the girls, speaking as if with one voice, had described this environment as unacceptable for their purpose. With an upswing in the business life of the area the station had become very crowded and noisy. These days travellers were in a hurry. Leisurely contact and discussions with promising clients were no longer easy and a shortage was growing in temporary accommodation likely to facilitate such encounters.

A number of the more intelligent and purposeful girls arranged a meeting at which it was agreed that they no longer wished to accost men who were weighed down

by baggage and usually in a hurry, and with that the
decision was made to move *en masse* to a more sedate
area in the vicinity.

The Corso Umberto was chosen. It is in what is
officially designated the historical centre of the city – a
place of splendid buildings now approaching decay, frequented by substantial bourgeois citizens, an occasional
police officer in ceremonial dress and a few priests
pecking at their coffee in sidewalk cafés. Here the mass
invasion by black *luccioli* produced a stunned outcry
among the resident population followed by endless telephone calls in protest to the nearest police headquarters.
The situation, thoroughly ventilated in the press, was to
produce surprising disclosures. It was, for example, discovered that the best business of the day, from the girls'
viewpoint, was negotiated with travellers who arrived
on the last train from Catania. They took them to the
ornamental gardens of the neighbouring Foro Italico,
from where, to use a picturesque police description, they
'turned into vapour' at dawn. The newspapers emphasized that this was not a wholly satisfactory solution
from the public health point of view.

Under pressure by local families the papers reported
that the nuisance factor was very great. Householders
complained of parading prostitutes accompanied by
young bloods laughing loudly and pounding their car-
horns in a way that made it impossible to sleep. The
police were charged with not doing their duty, and some
residents were said to be asking whether the Mafia might
not perhaps be called in to help. The suggestion throws
a revealing light on the Sicilian culture of these days in
which the Mafia is seen as not necessarily 'all bad', and
can sometimes be persuaded to come to the community's

assistance when, as in a case like this, the law appears as ineffective.

The problem in the 'historical centres' of cities like Syracuse and Palermo is poverty and overcrowding. Peasant families who have never forgotten the hard times of the feudal estates, abolished only when it was almost too late, crowd into the towns and will tolerate any living conditions rather than abandon the urban life to which they are now addicted. Poor families manage to squeeze themselves into the gaps in these gaunt and cracked, although once palatial, buildings. They put up shacks made from packing cases among the courtyards and one may find five girls sleeping in a shack fifteen feet square. Unfortunately these places stink like stables. Chief of Police Antonio Manganelli, calling again for tolerance and compassion, says that prostitution on a scale which hardly exists elsewhere in Europe is not curable. Nor, he adds, is it a crime according to Italian law. 'If prostitution were a crime I could organize drives and clear the streets of them. But it is not. On the other hand it is a social phenomenon that has taken control because of the strength of the demand.'

Roberta Torre's film is still considered a potential winner and pictures of her are frequently published. She appears as bespectacled, plumpish and petite with a caring and involved expression, directed particularly at Joey, whom she is determined to put on the road to success. It is unfortunate for her that the film project should have coincided with the *luccioli* invasion. However all is not lost with the Sicilian South Side Story, as there have been meetings with the Social Affairs Minister,

Livia Turco, who has raised hopes about the possibility of something being done to help both Joey and other potential artists who might find themselves trapped in her situation. From a discussion in September 1998 with the Hon. Turco, the news was that Article 16 of the Law 40/98 might be applied. In Joey's case this could mean the concession of a year's residence in Sicily 'for motives of social protection'. If this were to go through she would also receive the support of the Social Services Office during the period.

17

SFERRACAVALLO IS FIVE miles out of Palermo on the coast road to the west. It is the site of an ancient fishing settlement, and its present population, whatever their wealth or standing, is descended from the fisherfolk of the past, and, like them, psychologically influenced by the presence of the sea. On the whole they are tall people of notably bolder personality than the cultivators who live a few miles inland. Most of their fishing is done with lights at night, so they have developed the custom of having intercourse with their wives only during the afternoons. Unlike the neighbouring peasants they rarely save money but spend the cash as fast as they earn it, and customarily celebrate a good catch by lashing out on trinkets for the female members of their family. The fishermen are notorious gamblers and cases have been known of a man staking his house or even his wife on a bet. The basis of their relatively good fortune lies in the fact that while the rich have come into possession of almost every acre of land worth having, they have so far been unable to buy any part of the sea, which continues to be available to all and sundry. Apart from a house, and their boats and tackle, most fisherfolk are devoid of the burden of prosperity and thus wonderfully free.

Sicilian cultivators of the soil, on the other hand, have almost by tradition led hard lives in servitude to feudal estates. They have been exploited by the landowners, controlled by the Mafia, preyed upon until recently by bandits, and compelled to vote for the party of the Church. The best fortune that could befall any family was to have produced a son bright enough to have been trained as a priest. It is a solution avoided by the fisherfolk, who here, as in other coastal areas of Europe, are inclined to the practice of a discreet agnosticism. Having said that, I should at once point out that Sferracavallo is the site of a prodigious procession every autumn and whether it is based upon religious fervour or on a desire to celebrate the fruits of the harvest, there is nothing of the like to be experienced elsewhere in Sicily.

Saints Cosima and Damiano belonged while on earth to the medical profession and in the afterlife are seen locally as patron saints of the faith-healing practised here in its most successful form. From the moment that these two medieval effigies jog into view seated side by side on their float over the heads of the ecstatic crowd, spontaneous cures take place, and many cases have been recorded of the chronically sick, in biblical style, picking up their beds to walk. The saints' origins are obscure. There is said to have been a Saracenic school of medicine in the area a thousand or so years ago but it would be questionable to suggest that the two pink-cheeked Nordics carried in the procession could have had any connection with Islam. Apart from their fame as physicians, the saints protected their followers from a whole list of the normal hazards of their day. When sea-rovers raided Sferracavallo the images were carried out and a mere glimpse of the wrath on the saints' faces was enough to put them to flight. Damiano, a strong swimmer, set out on several occasions – in one instance assisted by a dolphin – to bring back survivors of boats wrecked in storms. Above all the two saints combined forces to defeat the great plague of 1624; while others were dying like flies, not a single inhabitant of Sferracavallo was lost.

Traditionally the great procession at Sferracavallo took place in the afternoon of the festival's first day, but now despite the protests of the old faithful of the town the saints are brought out only for show and the procession is staged after dark. To be in the select company of those who carry the *vara* – the platform upon which the saints are enthroned – it is required that the applicant shall be of unquestioned morality and 'take the oath'. In the old days, the procession set out to visit and convey hope to every person sick in bed throughout the town. Those who could be moved would be carried to a doorway or even placed at a window where they could see the saints' faces and listen to the prayers said for their cure. Whatever the state of these side-streets the carriers of the heavy float went barefoot, often leaving traces of blood. It was said that one in ten of the bedridden visited in this way found the strength to hoist themselves to their feet in order to bow their heads to the saints, and once in a while someone was cured on the spot and walked again from that time on.

Modern times put an end to these extraordinary scenes. Many people were ashamed at the idea of displaying the sick in this way as they did a hundred years ago. The general opinion was that the celebrations were out of touch with the times, so the traditional afternoon procession was cancelled and one took place only at night, and stuck to the shopping streets, thus depriving the sick of their comfort and hope. Pietro Assurrino, who had helped carry a float 'out of devotion for our protectors for over twenty-one years', was sad to confirm that nowadays the majority of the carriers were very young people. 'They decided to brighten things up,' he said, 'and they march as fast as they can. We still go barefoot, and a few of us still pray. The trouble is you can't hear the prayers for the noise of the band.'

I was told that a number of natives of Sferracavallo who had left for the United States during the last forty years did all they could to return to their home town for the procession, where they were welcomed by their friends from the old days. Their hosts listened entranced to the fluency of their English and were relieved to find that the visitors had no trouble expressing themselves in equally fluent Italian, sometimes even throwing in a few words of Sicilian dialect. The visitors described, to general astonishment, the marvels of such cities as Buffalo and Detroit, and were relieved to be assured that things back in Sicily were at least no worse than they had been. Among the novelties in Sferracavallo brought to the notice of the friends and relatives back from the States was the new craze for painting gigantic pictures of the 'Sainted Physicians' on the façades of some of the town's largest houses. The saints were shown wearing larger than usual crowns, their purple robes as before, but by way of a novelty, high laced-up boots like those worn by competitors in sporting events.

When the saints actually joined the procession they held between them a tray covered with gold-leaf supporting examples of the beakers, flasks, long-handled mirrors and intestinal pumps once commonly in use in the medical profession.

Many of the new arrivals had planned short tours to use up the now largely vacant first day of the festival, choosing the picturesque road by the sea leading to Castellammare, and intending to call in on any relative with whom they had remained in touch. All had hired the largest possible cars to be found in Palermo for the outing.

Several big houses along this road had put up notices offering hospitality to visitors from overseas, and by the time of our arrival a number of lunch parties were on the way. Being urged by Sicilian friends travelling with us to join one of them, we did so, finding ourselves at a table with a middle-aged man who had arrived on the previous day from Denver. I asked him about the great emigration after the war, and he said, 'Nothing pushed me into emigrating. I worked on the boats, but everyone was pulling out and I guess I just caught the mood.'

'Did you go back to the sea in the States?'

'There was no sea around to go back to. Folks of ours were living in Spokane and they fixed it for us to come on over. I went to work for an outfit in the building materials trade nearby, and round about twenty years later I took it over. It's really great to be back here. I come every year. Trouble is I have four grandchildren to think about these days, otherwise I'd like to stick around for a bit. You have to remember there's not the education here we're looking for. We're hoping to send all the kids to Galileo High.'

This was a very Sicilian scene. The people whose hospitality we were enjoying had handed round plates piled with spaghetti and they kept filling our glasses with wine that was quite black until you held it up to the light. A child had been given a hen to play with, and was dragging it about by a string tied round its leg. Sea-birds were mewing like kittens in the garden, which was half beach, and two tables away a priest with pink cheeks had nodded off to sleep and let out a single snore. About half the occupants of the room were Sicilians who had never left the island, and the rest had spent thirty or more years in the States and were an inch or two taller than those who had stayed at home. Those who had returned to pay their respects to the Sainted Physicians were also distinguishable by their flamboyant gestures, and listening to their constant outbursts of laughter one realized once again how very rare laughter was in the country of their birth.

Back in Sferracavallo numerous preparations for the night procession were under way. The faces, hands and feet of the saints were wiped with napkins of silk before being lifted tenderly into position on their pedestals to await the gilded tray with its medical paraphernalia. Among the fifty-five carriers chosen to make up the *vara* was Filippo Parco from Boston, aged twenty-four, a sufferer from depression who was here for the fifth year in succession, and who had been kept in the closest possible proximity with the images since their emergence from the chapel earlier in the day. When the procession was ready to move off, Filippo Parco would take his place in the centre of the front row of carriers directly under the beneficial gaze of both saints. It was a treatment found to be so successful that it only called for occasional topping-up by private visits to the chapel where the effigies spent the rest of the year.

Whether for religious or other reasons the procession was a most exciting affair for the majority of the town's population who took part. A twenty-eight-instrument brass band belted out an almost overpowering sound as it squeezed its way through crowds surging in the main street, and although many lips moved in prayer few of the words were audible. To me what was extraordinary was the number of visitors from overseas who left restaurant tables and burrowed into the crowd, holding up mobile phones to capture this moment for listeners in the States. 'For our friends and families back home,' said one of them, 'this is very important. We want them to share our joy. This is the great moment of our year.'

18

TO AN OLD Sicilian hand, as I believe myself to be, this is a Mediterranean island where the majority of public happenings are seen in one way or another to be bizarre. What, one wonders, can be amiss with a legal system in which Andreotti – prime minister seven times and suspected of connections with the murder of an antagonistic journalist – can be acquitted after a trial lasting four years during which he was seen to enjoy complete freedom of movement? How can it be that the murderous bandit Giuliano, although nominally in gaol, was taken on shopping expeditions by his gaolers, and to parties at the Archbishop's palace in Monreale? Or that Sicily's most notorious murderer, Totò Riina, has collected a record for the Italian State of twenty-three life sentences – none of which has been served? Even these episodes may seem less extraordinary than the news, published in the Sicilian press in autumn 1998, that a number of *capi-mafia* attending a conference in Palermo had taken advantage of the security provided by the Ucciardone prison to hold their 'constructive discussions' behind its protective walls. After a night's hospitality, said the report, they were released in the early hours next day. It was at this top-level conference that Giovanni Brusca, found guilty of ordering the murder by strangulation of the Di Matteo child, spoke with a kind of passion of the necessity of maintaining human values, and was assured by those present that this was the common aim.

It was an episode belonging to the period of hopeful renewal when the nation's optimists brought themselves to believe that even the Mafia could be changed for the better. November was here and with the first, fresh breezes of approaching winter the national mood firmed, and Sicilians put the muddle, the delays, and the petty strategies of summer behind them to prepare themselves for the coming year.

The end of the road had come for the 'sealed-off' old palaces awaiting demolition. Illicit tenants were flushed from their hiding places and the modern equivalent of battering rams knocked down the walls. It was the month when tax offices sent out final demands, petty offenders were released from prisons, shops got rid of old stock at any price and sacks of misaddressed correspondence were either burnt or emptied into the sea. Pigeons, now at their fattest, were netted or even caught by rod and line on the city roofs to be converted into *pâté di fin d'anno*, much in demand in the Christmas season.

With this, as is so often the case, a massive police drive against criminality of all kinds was planned and the two police forces reluctantly agreed to collaborate again, with the heads of the carabinieri and Pubblica Sicurezza exchanging kisses after a banquet arranged for them at the State's expense in the most famous of Palermo's Mafia-owned seafood restaurants.

This happy settlement of old scores was to provide the stage-setting for the biggest, the most carefully prepared, and certainly the most expensive police offensive in Sicilian history. It was to be known as *Grande Oriente* (Great Eastern), and was to be launched on four fronts in the east of the island where the Mafia now held sway in its latest, deadliest and most effective form. The Mafia commander-in-chief against whom the attack was to be launched was relatively unknown in Palermo but proved to be possibly one of the most remarkable Sicilians of his day.

Bernardo Provenzano lived under the protection of almost total anonymity. Only one picture had ever appeared of him in a newspaper. Taken at the time of his first arrest, it showed him as a boy of about eighteen who had perhaps been subjected to plastic surgery after a severe accident. Retouching had emptied this face of all expression. Now in his sixties, Provenzano was described as gaunt in appearance with deep furrows in his cheeks and tufts of white hair over his ears. He was an admirer of Saddam Hussein and was said to spend his spare time writing an account of the campaigns of Julius Caesar.

Back in the late eighties Marcello Cimino had taken me to an antique bookshop in the Via Roma and drawn my attention to a middle-aged man hunched over a book in the reading room. He whispered to me that this was Bernardo Provenzano – the most powerful private citizen, he said, in Sicily.

Provenzano, he later explained, had remained a fugitive from justice since his first boyhood arrest and had subsequently, over thirty years, broken all records for hyperactive criminality, having taken control of innumerable enterprises in the country. He remained invisible in the background of an organization run by a corps of carefully selected villains known as his 'colonels', forty-seven of whom were arrested in the course of the *Grande Oriente* operation. This, although carrying out a useful clean-up of such towns as Catania, fell short of expectations in that it failed to remove Provenzano himself from circulation.

One theory was that Sicily in effect needed this man because of the incomparable efficiency displayed in all his undertakings. All businesses coming under his control showed an immediate improvement in their performance, and there were many who hoped that some way might be found of putting his talents to good use in the service of the State. Shortly before the great police drive he had won the contract for a new system of roads for Piazza Armerina, where the loss of his services would probably have been seen as disappointing. He was known to keep a close eye on every aspect of his numerous commercial affairs, and to bombard his colonels with innumerable letters, hammered out on an old-fashioned typewriter, with which he kept them up to scratch. All these reflected his religious background in their literary style and began 'Dearest, in the hope that this finds you in the best of health', and ended 'May the Lord bless and protect you'. Important letters were composed by his wife and, among orders couched in military style, contained some reference to the goodness of the Almighty. In the opinion of the police Provenzano's ability to avoid capture over the years had depended upon the fact that all his letters were sent not by post, but delivered through a series of couriers. In this way a letter might travel in a zigzag fashion from one end of the island to the other before arriving at its destination.

Provenzano, it was generally assumed, was far too intelligent ever to be caught, and the accepted rumour was that he was now enjoying a rest-cure in Bagheria, which, as an admirer of Sicilian baroque architecture, he visited frequently, sometimes, it was said, even to be seen sketching the grotesques of the Villa Palagonia. Like Salvatore Lima, another top *mafioso*, who had dared to correct an assize judge, about to pass sentence, for his faulty quotation from Shakespeare, Provenzano held the classics in respect. He was known to possess only two intimate friends, both of them females approaching middle age. They were well-known intellectuals, one of them with a university degree in philosophy. The other, only recently released from prison, practised faith-healing and curative magic for which she made no charge. It was this lady, using her powers of divination, who unmasked the designs of Provenzano's only male confidant, Luigi Llardo, who had become alarmed by Provenzano's fearful energy and his obvious but risky intention of taking over every enterprise of importance in the country.

There had also been a growing coolness between the two men over the matter of a private extortion carried out by Llardo, 500 million lire of which had gone into his own pocket instead of being handed over to the clan. Llardo decided to play for safety by making a cautious approach to a senior police officer, Colonel Riccio, with whom the question of his acceptance as a collaborator with justice might be broached. Such confidential allies of the police were treated with every respect, guarded wherever they went, and in general lived pleasant lives.

The meeting between the two men was arranged by Riccio with considerable skill. Llardo was arrested on some trivial charge and, following their secret discussion, released on the grounds of ill health. It seems likely, however, that the alert and watchful Provenzano would have suspected a certain artificiality in this encounter, and been at the back of what happened next.

Leaving the colonel that night, Llardo was driven home, and was on the point of entering his house when a stranger waiting in the shadows emptied a pistol into his head.

If the results of the *Grande Oriente* operations had at first seemed hopeful, proof that the Mafia was undefeated was soon forthcoming. The latest news from the south of the island in 1998 was of an extraordinary deal made between the clans of Cosa Nostra and a local version of the Mafia few had heard of called the *Stidda*. If a confrontation threatened, it would be agreed to limit the number of casualties involved. Those concerned were natives of Gela, Nisceni and Vittoria – the first two rather dull little towns where there was little for the active young to do beyond playing computer games in the bars and planning ineffectual criminal coups. Vittoria, the third town, is something quite different, for it possesses several square miles of the finest market gardens on the island which through a splendid conjunction of climate and soil produce fruit such as peaches several weeks before they are marketed in quantity elsewhere in Sicily, and therefore fetch high prices. My own interest lay in the area's production of such rare wildflowers as terrestrial orchids, which flower in profusion wherever the original soil is left intact. These, indeed, proved to be spectacular.

Predictably, the productive market gardens had attracted Mafia attention to Vittoria, and eventually a proportion of the native population turned into *mafiosi*, enriching themselves by extortions imposed upon fruit-growers who were doing only too well. What, however, appears as quite new in a situation where opposing Mafia groups began, as expected, to come into collision, is that they should seek to impose restraints upon the damage inflicted when it came to armed conflict. Other intelligent safeguards on outright criminal activities were imposed in Vittoria. Leading lights among the clans were selected for employment in Caltanissetta and Catania, where they studied how up-to-date businesses were conducted with the object of employing the experience thus gained in the operations at home. From then on, when the time came to collect extortions a member of each clan was present to ensure that all was well and truly above board. Clan members were paid a family allowance while in prison – if married, nearly double the amount a bachelor received. It is interesting that at about this time Vittoria's highly respected *maga* (witch), previously employed to deal with the citizens' emotional problems, should have been pensioned off.

Despite a show of modernity in their organization, the Vittoria Mafia clans suffered from basic weaknesses due to a series of factors over which the predominantly young *mafiosi* had little control. Thus when a sudden and unexpected crisis arose safeguards went by the board. Vittoria was a small town, and probably without realizing it subject in every way to the influences of its powerful near-neighbour Catania – the culturally dominant town in eastern Sicily. Catania was 'extreme' in comparison to Cosa Nostra's 'moderates' in Palermo, and many of the town's numerous men of respect had been able to defend themselves a month earlier against the *Grande Oriente* operation, it turned out. Fatally, the mentality created by the extremists of Catania called not for conciliation but action in Vittoria. But Vittoria was small in population and resources, and with a lifestyle suited more to the moderation of Sicily's western clans than the Catania Mafia's ideal of the all-out attack. In addition to this, Vittoria suffered from a class-ridden society dominated by a small handful of 'old' families who had little contact with the majority of its people, and, besides cornering much of the local wealth, remained wholly aloof. Even in the case of the Mafia community of old where the *capo-mafia* and a few of his henchmen shared between them nine-tenths of the production of the land, these men had always been accessible to members of the lower class. In Vittoria the top families isolated themselves, and were thus exposed to the detestation of the underdogs.

On 2 January 1999 five feuding members of Cosa Nostra and *Stidda* were shot dead in the Esso bar in Vittoria, possibly, it has been suggested, on orders communicated by mobile telephone from Germany. It became clear from police investigations that the old-fashioned Sicilian Mafia was becoming steadily more international in character. Suspects picked up by the police spoke of foreign connections. It was clear that even in Sicily – still in so many ways encased in its primeval traditions – change could come about. Even the attack in the Esso bar had been a highly modernized version of the old gang warfare, this time fought with mobile phones and Kalashnikovs. Christmas festivities were hardly at an end and the first reporter to arrive after the shoot-out noted the large luminous sign *Buon Natale* was still over the bar's door.

A few days later simultaneous funeral services were conducted in two of Vittoria's churches. It was instantly apparent that the town's tragedy had done nothing to draw the members of a divided community closer together. Huge public resentment was shown when half an hour before the cortège formed by the two leading families, Motta and Mirabella, was due to arrive at the gates of the Cathedral of St John, these were closed to everyone else to make certain of the exclusion of any member of what is known in Sicily as 'the family classes'. This almost produced a riot in the main square by groups of youths who screamed abuse at the privileged mourners under the protection of the police.

For the rest it was to be the lesser Church of the Sacred Heart, a fine baroque building, although devoid on such occasions of prestige. Vittoria is a city obsessed by football, and within minutes of the opening of the doors the church was packed with players in the colours of their local team, a group even chanting its anthem against the hardly audible dirge of those who had come there to mourn.

Inside the cathedral, the Motta and Mirabella families gathered in a small, silent group in the shadows of the majestic nave to listen to a suitable homily delivered by its archpriest, Giuseppe Cali, who addressed the two dead man in their coffins in an easy and familiar way, as if they were still able to follow his logic. 'Claudio and Angelo,' he began, 'society has been unable to come to your rescue.' He made use of the kind of familiarity permissible in the case of a close relative. 'As a boy I remember once giving you a smacking. In the way a father does to his son. An affectionate reprimand. Nothing more.'

19

WITH THE SOUND of bells at midnight 1998 reached its end. It had been notorious for excesses of all kinds. Even the weather had been extraordinary; in February hot sunshine had driven city sun-worshippers to the beaches, while in August torrential rain sent muddy flood water coursing down the capital's streets. This was a year in which Lo Zingaro, the nature reserve overlooking the island's northern shore, had come under attack by obviously demented arsonists on no less than four occasions. Mysterious superficial damage had been inflicted upon the marvellous Roman mosaics of Piazza Armerina, the last of these acts of vandalism within weeks of the New Year. The bronze effigy known as 'The Dancing Satyr', recovered from the waters of Mazara del Valo after an immersion of 2,500 years, had eventually been surrendered to Rome following a national dispute as to where it was to be housed. An eruption of Stromboli, at least three years in advance of the time when it was calculated to take place, caused a four-fold increase in the insurance premiums of fashionable people living in that area.

Of the ten thousand or so illegal immigrants who had discovered means of entering the island in 1998, a hundred, it was said, had actually arrived by helicopter. A few of these, and others picked up by the police, had been served with expulsion orders, but the general belief was that the rest were in the process of being absorbed into the local population, and that their offspring would rate as Sicilians.

The *mafiosi*, for whom above all else the island was famous, had had a good year, with prominent figures such as Vitale of the enormous telescope fame still in the limelight. After a trial in which a life sentence had been confidently predicted he had been released due to insufficient evidence.

For the first time in his existence Totò Riina had actually been found *not* guilty in a criminal court. Charged with the murder of Judge Scopelliti, he had been instantly freed, instead of going through the farce of a guilty verdict which would then be quashed. For all his crimes, Sicily's supreme murderer had in fact remained as free as air for much of his long life.

In 1980, when I had spent some weeks touring the island with Marcello, I asked about the possibility of meeting with Riina. 'In this part of the civilized world anything can be arranged,' he replied. I laughed and he said, 'It's something you should know well by now. It costs a donation to one of the churches – I believe through some kind of religious agency.'

'How much?'

'Several million last time it came up in conversation, a year or so ago. It's almost certainly more by now. Another thing is that he's a man of habit. He goes for a morning walk at the same time every day up the same two or three streets, and that's the only time when he'll talk to you. If you're interested I'm sure that's another case where an agent's involved. You pay a million or two for five minutes' chat and the agent tells you what you can say and what you can't. Riina is always well wrapped up against the cold, so you see practically nothing of his face. No photographs, I should add. It hardly seems worthwhile, does it?'

'I agree,' I said.

Finally, this was the year when the Vatican had condemned the return to Sicily – and to the Italian mainland itself – of the local witches and exorcists known as *maghi*. These had reappeared in their hundreds in areas either where no doctors were in practice, or where the sick were unable to scrape together the money to pay their fees.

In Sicily low incomes and ignorance have protected simple beliefs. The peasantry pay little attention to astrologers and their stars, and are lukewarm in attitude even to conventional religion. In many cases a *maga* provides the well-tried old remedies and will stroke a sick child's brows with healing fingers in return for a couple of slices of bread. For those who can afford the outlay, few maladies can resist a cock's throat cut for a few coins, and a little of the blood rubbed well into the roots of the tongue. Should the *maga* be from Nigeria – as many are these days – she will carve a neat little pattern designed to ward off the evil eye in the skin on the small of the back or between the breasts. All that is needed is the ability to believe; the *maga's* power is to call this tiny geyser of acceptance and hope to life in the depths of her patient's soul.

20

WE ARE ALL drawn by the magnet of the sea. Boys born within sound of the waves long to be ship's captains, or at least fishermen. The child released on holiday from buildings and streets stares entranced at the purity of the rocks, waves and the deserted beach, and reluctantly rejoins parents to be led back to house-confinement. In his imagination the Sicilian child steers a boat through uncharted waters or lends a hand to haul in a net full of fish. These are pleasures inherited from the past which few will ever enjoy.

If the sea itself is now beyond reach for everyday involvement, the next best thing may be settling in a town by the sea. Such towns are inclined to be more animated, more attuned to pleasure and less involved in the dullness of commerce and industry than those of the interior. The heart of the inland city will almost certainly be an ebullient and traffic-congested central square. The life of the coastal town is normally concentrated along the shore of the sea's great oasis of calm, and few urban areas exist where it is simpler to relax.

In Sicily

Palermo is well sited and rich enough to possess both attributes. Its city-centre traffic is infernal, but the gardens, ancient palaces, squares and promenades down by the water place it in a class of its own. The traditional centre of the city at the Quattro Canti is linked to the port area by the dead-straight mile of the Corso Vittorio Emanuele, but many visitors take a short cut through a maze of side-streets as complicated as any on earth.

Down by 'the water', as the port is called, a man in a hurry who has slipped through the labyrinth of the old town is about to enter another world. The wind in the salt marsh ahead veers round with a temperature drop of several degrees. With this the odours of the Vucciria market are blown away, and only the faintest whiff of farm animals remains. As the port comes closer a landscape of the far past is lost, and ahead the profiles of magnificent churches rise from the flatlands into the clear sky. The Piazza Marina, coming into sight, is perhaps the most interesting square in Palermo, the whole of its vast area being surrounded by palaces slowly approaching decay. Of these the largest is the huge Palazzo Chiaramonte – for a century the headquarters of the Inquisition – a sinister building flanked by the splendid Renaissance church of Santa Maria dei Miracoli.

This is the homeland of the traditional Sicily of wealth, creative genius, and the monstrous powers of Church and State. A human aspect of local life has been preserved in the Piazza as in so many other open spaces. Here in the cool of the evening among the pleasant muddle of eastern Palermo, the elderly citizens carry out their green baize tables to enjoy a game of cards. Above all, the port area is given up to leisure and display. Smiling Tunisians pour cups of the world's best coffee. The florists are at their stalls embowered in the costliest flowers. The doorman at a prestigious hotel rushes out to assure guests arriving by car that it will be safe to leave it unlocked. There is even a magnificently cool and calm hospital on the sea front, of which Lesley, having been treated there *free of charge* for her damaged hand, speaks with utmost praise.

On the eve of our departure, we had been invited by some friends to join them for a farewell lunch somewhere on the front. We thus became components of the maritime scene to which the crowds are attracted on fine weekends. All the usual participants were present, some dressed in slightly nautical styles suited to the occasion. A handsome young priest who strode past in a black soutane was by no means out of place. Nor was a carabinieri *maresciallo*, inscrutably watchful from a street corner, nor certainly the stylish lady in control of three quarrelsome dogs. We moved towards the agreed meeting place with little idea of where the restaurant could be. In Palermo, all the best places to eat in are tucked away down backstreets where the rents are low and the owner can afford to splash out on the quality of his food. The Sicilian diner has long trained himself to ignore dreary surroundings in the knowledge that a sea-view will double the bill. Entering the restaurant of his choice, he is inspired by the confidence that the fish brought to his table will often have been caught on the same day, thus providing a gastronomic experience calling for appetite alone.

A stroll to the end of the promenade was enough to

convince us that this was not a place for gastronomic surprises. We were there to see and be seen. People scrutinized each other conscientiously. A man unwrapped a telescope and focused it on the passengers on the deck of the nearest ship, and a respectful crowd gathered nearby as a TV crew went into action, calling upon onlookers with anything exceptional in their appearance to say a few words.

Owing to the density of the weekend crowd we had had some difficulty in locating our friends, but further on, where the Foro Italico follows the seashore and the crowd thins, we ran into them. As it transpired, the occasion for our last outing together had been particularly well chosen, for two of our friends had just had good news. Carolina, who worked for the Banco di Sicilia, had heard on only the previous day of a promotion, and almost simultaneously Giuseppe, a struggling author, had at last found a publisher for his book.

The third member of our party, Agostino, had long since been freed to some extent from the immediate necessity of windfalls of this kind. For owing to a tremendous stroke of luck some five years before, he had become one of six top prize-winners in the Superenatallo lottery, enriching him by the equivalent of almost a million pounds. He had immediately given up work, explaining to his friends that all he hoped to do from that time on was to learn to think more clearly. Nevertheless he had also taken time to brush up his fluency in several languages, and like our other two Sicilian friends spoke English almost as well as a native of our country.

'So where are we going, then?' Carolina asked.

'I forgot to tell you,' Giuseppe said. 'The news is good. One of my favourite restaurants has opened up again, so I thought we might go there. I managed to book the last table they had for lunch.'

'Why had it closed?' asked Agostino.

'They got caught by the police fiddling bills to get out of paying income tax. They couldn't buy their way out.'

'The story is they were also in trouble for having protected fish on the menu,' Carolina said. 'It was in the *Giornale.*'

'Anyway, the main thing is they're open, and I thought we might as well go over there before the police move in on them again,' Giuseppe said.

'When you say "protected fish" you mean *neonati*, don't you?' Agostino asked.

'Right, *neonati.*'

I asked what sort of fish this was, and Giuseppe explained that it was a kind of spawn taken in special ultra-fine nets only a few days after hatching out. 'I think you call them small fry,' he said. To this, Agostino, who was cynical in such matters, added, 'Three restaurants out of four will cook them for you on the quiet. Your people just weren't fast enough with the protection money, that's all.' Turning to Lesley, he said, 'Laws don't really exist in this country.'

At that moment the restaurant came into sight. It was a large blue cube of a building with seagulls in flight painted all over its façade. We agreed this was a disastrous intrusion upon an otherwise unspoilt and almost romantic seaside environment. There were about twenty cars, most of them German, in the car park, and a Tunisian in farcical pseudo-oriental garments welcomed us at the door. We went in and a stern-faced employee checked our identities and led us to a table. 'Unfriendly here, aren't they?' Agostino said.

'They have to be,' Giuseppe told him. 'They have to pretend to be *mafiosi,* even if they aren't. It's all part of the scene.'

'But why do people come here?'

'Because it's smart. If you call a superboss by his first name it impresses your friends.'

'What was the waiter writing on the pad?' Agostino asked, and Giuseppe told him: 'Our order.'

'But we haven't given him one,' Agostino said.

'It wasn't necessary. There is a standard menu. He just took a look at us and decided how much we'd pay.'

'So what are we getting? *Neonati*?'

'Right. They just brought them for the people at the next table, so that will be our first course, too.'

'Surely we can refuse it,' Carolina said. 'Can't we tell them that we didn't order whatever it is, and please take it away?'

'Not here,' Giuseppe said. 'The way they see it is, you come here, you're on their side. You leave the food – it's an insult. They're quick to take offence.'

Nevertheless, when the waiter came with the *neonati*, Agostino put it to one side. The boss, who was behind the waiter, stood back and watched. His face was smooth and red and expressionless, like the faces at Ficuzza, and like them, he probably rarely, if ever, smiled.

The hubbub of chatter around the tables in our vicinity had quietened as the diners sensed the unusual tension in the periphery of their well-regulated lives. My impression now was that the fury lurking in the boss's face that I had at first taken to be directed at us was in fact a permanent feature of his expression. Lips compressed and cheeks aflame, he turned and went off and the waiter took the *neonati* away. The slaughter of the innocents was clearly a feature of the cuisine, for the next course displayed the tiny limbs of a newborn lamb. It proved to possess such delicacy of flavour that it was regrettably easy to overcome shame. It was no wonder that the place's regular customers had found a way to keep it in business.

With the meal at an end the time had come for fond farewells, for Carolina was obliged to put in an appearance at her office before closing-time at the bank. A car had been sent to pick her up and the others decided to take advantage of a lift back to the centre. This left us with the rest of the afternoon free, and we decided to visit the eastern outskirts of the capital, which were reported as being of exceptional interest.

We managed to pick up a taxi which drove us across the network of roads leading into the capital from the east, finally dropping us near Villagrande. It was a region where the countryside still encroached on the outer suburbs of Palermo, and was said to be remarkably unchanged since the beginning of the century. The city's exhausted expansion had left no more than a scattering of modern buildings among untended fields in which scrubby bushes and even the odd misshapen tree had survived. The stillness here seemed to be emphasized by the soft orchestration of the traffic in the Corso a mile or so away. Ten years back ex-villagers who had taken employment in the city still rode on their bicycles to work. Their little grey houses with tiny windows out of reach from the ground were still there and in good shape. Some of the present occupants had gone in for a few yards of walled garden with a row of spikes set into the top bricks.

These people had remained country folk, happy to forfeit the regularities and benefits of urban life, the set hours of work, the exactitudes of pay and pensions, and the medical care. By contrast certain pleasures had survived, long lost elsewhere when the city houses closed in. They grew vines in these back gardens, producing each year a few bottles of sweet and invigorating white wine, celebrated all the feasts, married virgins and reared for the market those long-legged cockerels strutting so confidently in the streets of the Vucciria on their way to their doom.

Here we were on the frontier of two versions of civilization, as recently reported upon by the sociologist Professor Angelo Reina. In the depressed outskirts of Palermo, he noted, adults had lost on average three-quarters of a centimetre in height over a decade – as a result he believed of deprivation of light. Villagers colonizing semi-deserted areas such as this had actually become three-quarters of a centimetre taller during the same period, benefiting, he believed, from 'unofficial cultivation' – meaning take-overs of abandoned land – which had enabled them to improve their diet.

We stopped at a miscellaneous collection of hutments and half-built houses, named, according to a noticeboard, *Conforto* – Comfort. After a chat with a group of its natives who came into sight, this seemed not an unreasonable description. They were clearly delighted and stimulated by strange faces in their midst, and they seized on this excuse to put aside whatever they were doing and gather round for a chat. The dialect here was a difficult one, but a gleeful veteran with understandable Italian made his approach, dragging a piglet on a lead. We had seen no farms in the area – what did people do for a living? I asked, and his smile widened. They grew vegetables, he said, including the longest zucchini in Sicily, which they exchanged for meat. They hoped to develop tourism. There were caves at the back of the village where cavemen once lived, and one of these contained a portion of fossilized bear.

Were they ever troubled by the Mafia? I asked, and the man laughed at the idea. 'We're poor,' he said, and it sounded like a boast. 'Why should they bother with us? The Mafia feeds on the rich. We've never set eyes on one. Sometimes the carabinieri send a collector for a contribution to their funds and we give him a few onions. There's no money here to pay for doctors, but the *mago* casts a spell and gets the same result for a couple of cabbages. The nearest school is ten kilometres away so he teaches the kids arithmetic while he's about it.'

A small boy passed, whistling, with golden wings attached to his shoulders. 'It's for his saint's day,' the old man explained. 'Something they make a big fuss of here. The family and a few friends will eat rabbit tonight. Why don't you stay with us and wish him a long life?'

Thanking him, I explained to him that we were on our way to Punta Raisi to catch a plane.

'Pity,' he said. 'If you come back this way don't fail to stop and give us your news.'

I assured him that we would and a long handshake in the old-fashioned Sicilian style followed before I signalled to the driver to start up, and we moved off. It had been an experience that renewed the memory of the good fellowship and the dignity of the Sicilian countryside which had remained for so many years unchallenged in the mind's eye, and I knew that once again I would leave the island with regret.

Thank you for flying
Northwest Airlines. Please retain
this portion of your boarding pass.

Visit us online at **nwa.com**
for all your travel planning needs,
from Frequent Flyer information
and award travel reservations to
flight status, schedules, availability
and pricing.

Dear Customer, please take a moment to provide contact information.

1. Contact Name _____

2. Contact Phone Number _____

   (Include country code, area code and number)

   (A person not traveling with you today)

3. **Are you a U.S. Citizen?**   Yes ☐   No ☐

4. I decline to provide this information. ☐

This information is only retained for 24 hours and will remain confidential. Thank you.

NORTHWEST AIRLINES — E-TICKET

CONNECTION

Name: HAWKINS/WILLIAM.E.MR
Date: 06MAY03   Conf #: 3CDPS5
Frequent Flyer Nbr: Request:
E-Ticket Nbr: E012218702261
Flight: NW1134

Gate: Seat: 41-C

Depart: Detroit   6:53AM
Arrive: Baltimore   8:22AM

BOARDING PASS

NORTHWEST AIRLINES — E-TICKET

CONNECTION

Name: HAWKINS/WILLIAM.E.MR
Date: 06MAY03   Conf #: 3CDPS5
Frequent Flyer Nbr: Request:
E-Ticket Nbr: E012218702261
Flight: NW1134

Gate: Seat: 41-C

Depart: Detroit   6:53AM
Arrive: Baltimore   8:22AM

Index

Index

Index